CHARLES DICKENS

AS A READER.

BY

CHARLES KENT.

PHILADELPHIA:
J. B. LIPPINCOTT & CO.
LONDON: CHAPMAN & HALL, 193, PICCADILLY.
1872.

LONDON:
BRADBURY, EVANS, AND CO., PRINTERS, WHITEFRIARS.

TO

JOHN FORSTER,

THE BIOGRAPHER OF CHARLES DICKENS,

These Pages are Inscribed.

PREFACE.

As the title-page of this volume indicates, no more is here attempted than a memorial of CHARLES DICKENS in association with his Readings. It appeared desirable that something in the shape of an accurate record should be made of an episode in many respects so remarkable in the career of the most popular author of his generation. A commemorative volume, precisely of this character, was projected by the writer in the spring of 1870. Immediately after the Farewell Reading in St. James's Hall, on the 15th of March, CHARLES DICKENS wrote, in hearty approval of the suggestion, "Everything that I can let you have in aid of the proposed record (which, *of course*, would be far more agreeable to me if done by you than by any other hand) shall be at your service." All the statistics, he added, should be placed freely at the writer's command; all the marked books from which he himself read should be confided to him for reference. In now realising his long-postponed intention, the writer's endeavour has been throughout to restrict the purpose of his book as much as possible to matters either directly or indirectly affecting these famous Readings.

The Biography of CHARLES DICKENS having been undertaken by the oldest and dearest of his friends, all that is here attempted is to portray, as accurately as may be, a single phase in the career and character of one of the greatest of all our English Humorists. What is thus set forth has the advantage, at any rate, of being penned from the writer's own intimate knowledge. With the Novelist's career as a Reader he has been familiar throughout. From its beginning to its close he has regarded it observantly. He has viewed it both from before and from behind the scenes, from the front of the house as well as from within the shelter of the screen upon the platform. When contrasted with the writings of the Master-Humorist, these readings of his, though so remarkable in themselves, shrink, no doubt, to comparative insignificance. But simply considering them as supplementary, and, certainly, as very exceptional, evidences of genius on the part of a great author, they may surely be regarded as having been worthy of the keenest scrutiny at the time, and entitled afterwards to some honest commemoration.

CONTENTS.

CHARLES DICKENS

AS

A READER.

A CELEBRATED writer is hardly ever capable as a Reader of doing justice to his own imaginings. Dr. Johnson's whimsical anecdote of the author of The Seasons admits, in point of fact, of a very general application. According to the grimly humorous old Doctor, "He [Thomson] was once reading to Doddington, who, being himself a reader eminently elegant, was so much provoked by his odd utterance, that he snatched the paper from his hand, and told him that he did not understand his own verses!" Dryden, again, when reading his Amphytrion in the green-room, "though," says Cibber, who was present upon the occasion, "he delivered the plain meaning of every period, yet the whole was in so cold, so flat, and unaffecting a manner, that I am afraid of not being believed when I affirm it." Elsewhere, in his Apology, when contrasting the creator with the interpreter, the original delineator with the actual impersonator of character, the same old stage gossip remarks, how men would read Shakspere with higher rapture could they but conceive how he was played by Betterton! "Then might they know," he exclaims, with a delightful extravagance of emphasis and quaintness of phraseology, "the one was born alone to speak what the other only knew to write!" The simple truth of the matter being that for the making of a consummate actor, reader, or impersonator, not only is there required, to begin with, a certain histrionic instinct or dramatic aptitude, but a combination—very rarely to be met with, indeed—of personal gifts, of physical peculiarities, of vocal and facial, nay, of subtly and yet instantly appreciable characteristics. Referring merely to those who are skilled as conversationalists, Sir Richard Steele remarks, very justly, in the *Spectator* (No. 521), that, "In relations, the force of the expression lies very often more in the look, the tone of voice, or the gesture, than in the words themselves, which, being repeated in any other manner by the undiscerning, bear a very different interpretation from their original meaning." Whatever is said as to all that is requisite in the delivery of an oration by the master of all oratory, applies with equal distinctness to those who are readers or actors professionally. All depends on the countenance, is the *dictum* of Cicero,* and even in that, he says, the eyes bear sove-

* *De Oratore* iii., 59.

reign sway. Elsewhere, in his great treatise, referring to what was all-essential in oratorical delivery, according to Demosthenes, Tully, by a bold and luminous phrase, declares Action to be, as it were, the speech of the body,—"quasi sermo corporis." Voice, eyes, bearing, gesture, countenance, each in turn, all of them together, are to the spoken words, or, rather than that, it should be said, to the thoughts and emotions of which those articulate sounds are but the winged symbols, as to the barbed and feathered arrows are the bowstring. How essential every external of this kind is, as affording some medium of communication between a speaker and his auditors, may be illustrated upon the instant by the rough and ready argument of the *reductio ad absurdum.* Without insisting, for example, upon the impossibility of having a speech delivered by one who is actually blind, and deaf, and dumb, we need only imagine here its utterance, by some wall-eyed stammerer, who has a visage about as wooden and inexpressive as the figure-head of a merchantman. Occasionally, it is true, physical defects have been actually conquered, individual peculiarities have been in a great measure counteracted, by rhetorical artifice, or by the arts of oratorical delivery: instance the lisp of Demosthenes, the stutter of Fox, the brogue of Burke, and the burr of Brougham.

Sometimes, but very rarely, it has so happened that an actor of nearly peerless excellence, that a reader of all but matchless power, has achieved his triumphs, has acquired his reputation, in very despite of almost every conceivable personal disadvantage. Than the renowned actor already mentioned, for example, Thomas Betterton, a more radiant name has hardly ever been inscribed upon the roll of English players, from Burbage to Garrick. Yet what is the picture of this incomparable tragedian, drawn by one who knew him and who has described his person for us minutely, meaning Antony Aston, in his theatrical pamphlet, called the Brief Supplement? Why it is absolutely this,—"Mr. Betterton," says his truthful panegyrist, "although a superlative good actor, laboured under an ill figure, being clumsily made, having a great head, a short, thick neck, stooped in the shoulders, and had fat, short arms, which he rarely lifted higher than his stomach. He had little eyes and a broad face, a little pock-fretten, a corpulent body, and thick legs, with large feet. His voice was low and grumbling. He was incapable of dancing, even in a country dance." And so forth! Yet this was the consummate actor who was regarded by the more discerning among his contemporaries, but most of all by the brother actors who were immediately around him, as simply inimitable and unapproachable.

There was John Henderson, again, great in his time, both as a tragic and a comic actor, greatest of all as a reader or an impersonator. Hear him described by one who has most carefully and laboriously written his encomium, that is to say, by John Ireland, his biographer. What do we read of him? That in height he was below the common standard, that his frame was uncompacted, that his limbs were short and ill-proportioned, that his countenance had little of that flexibility which anticipates the tongue, that his eye had scarcely anything of that language which, by preparing the spectator for the coming sentence, enchains the attention, that his voice was neither silvery nor mellifluous. Nevertheless, by a subtlety of discrimination, that seemed almost intuitive, by a force of judgment and a fervency of mind, that were simply exquisite and irresistible, this was the very man who could at any moment, by an inflection of his voice or by the syncope of a chuckle, move his audience at pleasure to tears or to laughter. He could haunt their memories for years afterwards with the infinite tenderness of his ejaculation as Hamlet, of "The fair Ophelia!" He could convulse them with merriment by his hesitating utterance as Falstaff of "A shirt—and a half!" Incidentally it is remarked by the biographer of Henderson that the qualifications requisite to constitute a reader of especial excellence seem to be these, "a good ear, a voice capable of inflexion, an understanding of, and taste for, the beauties of the author." Added to this, there must be, of course, a feeling, an ardour, an enthusiasm sufficient at all times to ensure their rapid and vivid manifestation. Richly endowed in this way, however, though Henderson was, his gifts were weighted, as we have seen were those also of Betterton, by a variety of physical defects, some of which were almost painfully conspicuous. Insomuch was this the case, in the latter instance, that Tony Aston has oddly observed, in regard to the all but peerless tragedian, "He was better to meet than to follow; for his aspect [the writer evidently means, here, when met] was serious, venerable, and majestic; in his latter time a little paralytic." Accepting at once as reasonable and as accurate what has thus been asserted by those who have made the art of elocution their especial and chosen study for analysis, it is surely impossible not to recognise at a glance how enormously a reader must, by necessity, be advantaged, who, in addition to the intellectual and emotional gifts already enumerated, possesses those personal attributes and physical endowments in which a reader, otherwise of surpassing excellence, like Henderson, and an actor, in other respects of incomparable ability, like Betterton, was each in turn so glaringly deficient.

Whatever is here said in regard to Charles Dickens, it should be borne in mind, is written and published during the lifetime of his own immediate contemporaries. He himself, his readings, the sound of his voice, the ring of his footstep, the glance of his eye, are all still vividly within the recollection of the majority of those who will examine the pages of this memorial. Everything, consequently, which is set forth in them is penned with a knowledge of its inevitable revision or endorsement by the reader's own personal remembrance. It is in the full glare of that public remembrance that the present writer refers to the great novelist as an impersonator of his more remarkable creations. Everybody who has seen him, who has heard him, who has carefully watched him, though it may be but at a single one of these memorable readings, will recognise at a glance the accuracy or the inaccuracy of the delineation.

It is observable, in the first instance, in regard to Charles Dickens, that he had in an extraordinary degree the dramatic element in his character. It was an integral part of his individuality. It coloured his whole temperament or idiosyncracy. Unconsciously he described himself, to a T, in Nicholas Nickleby. "There's genteel comedy in your walk and manner, juvenile tragedy in your eye, and touch-and-go farce in your laugh," might have been applied to himself in his buoyant youth quite as readily and directly as to Nicholas. The author, rather than the hero of Nickleby, seems, in that happy utterance of the theatrical manager, to have been photographed. It cannot but now be apparent that, as an unpremeditated preliminary to Dickens's then undreamt-of career as a reader of his own works in public and professionally, the Private Theatricals over which he presided during several years in his own home circle as manager, prepared the way no less directly than his occasional Readings, later on, at some expense to himself (in travelling and otherwise) for purely charitable purposes. His proclivity stagewards, in effect, the natural trending of his line of life, so to speak, in the histrionic or theatrical direction, was, in another way, indicated at a yet earlier date, and not one jot less pointedly. It was so, we mean, at the very opening of his career in authorship, when having just sprung into precocious celebrity as the writer of the Sketches and of the earlier numbers of Pickwick, he contributed an opera and a couple of farces with brilliant success to the boards of the St. James's Theatre. Braham and Parry and Hullah winged with melody the words of "The Village Coquettes;" while the quaint humour of Harley excited roars of laughter through the whimsicalities of "Is She His Wife?" and "The Strange Gentleman." Trifles light as air though these effusions might be, the radiant bubbles showed even then, as by a casual freak which way with him the breeze in his leisure hours was drifting. A dozen years or more after this came the private theatricals at Tavistock House. Beginning simply, first of all, with his direction of his children's frolics in the enacting of a burletta, of a Cracker Bonbon for Christmas, and of one of Planché's charming fairy extravaganzas, these led up in the end through what must be called circuitously Dickens's emendations of O'Hara's version of Fielding's burlesque of "Tom Thumb," to the manifestation of the novelist's remarkable genius for dramatic impersonation: first of all, as Aaron Gurnock in Wilkie Collins's "Lighthouse," and afterwards as

Richard Wardour in the same author's "Frozen Deep." Already he had achieved success, some years earlier, as an amateur performer in characters not essentially his own, as, for example, in the representation of the senile blandness of Justice Shallow, or of the gasconading humours of Captain Bobadil. Just, as afterwards, in furtherance of the interests of the Guild of Literature and Art, he impersonated Lord Wilmot in Lytton's comedy of "Not so Bad as we Seem," and represented in a series of wonderfully rapid transformations the protean person of Mr. Gabblewig, through the medium of a delightful farce called "Mr. Nightingale's Diary." Whoever witnessed Dickens's impersonation of Mr. Gabblewig, will remember that it included a whole cluster of grotesque creations of his own. Among these there was a stone-deaf old man, who, whenever he was shouted at, used to sigh out resignedly, "Ah, it's no use your whispering!" Besides whom there was a garrulous old lady, in herself the worthy double of Mrs. Gamp; a sort of half-brother to Sam Weller; and an alternately shrieking and apologetic valetudinarian, who was, perhaps, the most whimsical of them all. Nothing more, however, need here be said in regard to Charles Dickens's share, either in these performances for the Guild or in the other strictly private theatricals. They are simply here referred to, as having prepared the way by practice, for the Readings, still so called, though, in all save costume and general *mis en scene,* they were from first to last essentially and intensely dramatic representations.

Readings of this character, it is curious to reflect for a moment, resemble somewhat in the simplicity of their surroundings the habitual stage arrangements of the days of Shakspere. The arena, in each instance, might be described accurately enough as a platform, draped with screens and hangings of cloth or of green baize. The principal difference, in point of fact, between the two would be apparent in this, that whereas, in the one case any reasonable number of performers might be grouped together simultaneously, in the other there would remain from first to last before the audience but one solitary performer. He, however, as a mere matter of course, by the very necessity of his position, would have to be regarded throughout as though he were a noun of multitude signifying many. Slashed doublets and trunk hose, might just possibly be deemed by some more picturesque, if not in outline, at least in colour and material, than the evening costume of now-a-days. But, apart from this, whatever would meet the gaze of the spectator in either instance would bear the like aspect of familiarity or of incongruity, in contrast to or in association with, the characters represented at the moment before actual contemporaries. These later performances partake, of course, in some sense of the nature of a monologue. Besides which, they involve the display of a desk and a book instead of the almost ludicrous exhibition of a board inscribed, as the case might be, "Syracuse" or "Verona." Apart from this, however, a modern reading is, in the very nature of it, like a reverting to the primitive simplicity of the stage, when the stage, in its social influences, was at its highest and noblest, when, for the matter of that, it was all but paramount. Given genius in the author and in the impersonator, and that very simplicity has its enormous advantages.

The greatest of all the law-givers of art in this later civilisation has more than merely hinted at what is here maintained. Goethe has said emphatically, in Wilhelm Meister, that a really good actor makes us soon enough forget the awkwardness, even the meanness, of trumpery decorations; whereas, he continues, a magnificent theatre is precisely the very thing that makes us feel the most keenly the want of actors of real excellence.* How wisely in this Goethe, according to his wont, has spoken, we all of us, here in England, know by our own experience. Of the truth of his opinion we have had in this country, of late years, more than one startling illustration. Archæological knowledge, scenic illusion, gorgeous upholstery, sumptuous costumes, have, in the remembrance of many, been squandered in profusion upon the boards of one of our London theatres in the getting up of a drama by the master-dramatist. All this has tended,

* "Ein guter schauspieler macht uns bald eine elende, unschickliche dekoration vergessen, dahingegen das schonste theater den mangel an guten schauspielern erst recht fuhlbar macht."

however, only to realise the more painfully the inadequacy of the powers, no less of the leading star than of his whole company, to undertake the interpretation of the dramatic masterpiece. The spectacle which we are viewing in such an instance is, no doubt, resplendent; but it is so purely as a spectacle. Everything witnessed is—

"So coldly sweet, so deadly fair,
We start, for soul is wanting there."

The result naturally is, that the public is disillusioned and that the management is bankrupt. Another strikingly-contrasted experience of the present generation is this, that, without any decorations whatever, enormous audiences have been assembled together, in the old world and in the new, upon every occasion upon which they have been afforded the opportunity, to hear a story related by the lips of the writer of it. And they have been so assembled not simply because the story itself (every word of it known perfectly well beforehand) was worth hearing again, or because there was a very natural curiosity to behold the famous author by whom it had been penned; but, above all, because his voice, his glance, his features, his every movement, his whole person, gave to his thoughts and his emotions, whether for tears or for laughter, the most vivid interpretation.

How it happened, in this instance, that a writer of celebrity like Charles Dickens became a reader of his own works before large public audiences may be readily explained. Before his first appearance in that character professionally—that is, as a public reader, on his own account—he had enjoyed more than twenty years of unexampled popularity as a novelist. During that period he had not only securely established his reputation in authorship, but had evidenced repeatedly, at intervals during the later portion of it, histrionic powers hardly less remarkable in their way than those gifts which had previously won for him his wholly exceptional fame as a writer of imagination.

Among his personal intimates, among all those who knew him best, it had long come to be recognised that his skill as an impersonator was only second to his genius as a creator of humorous and pathetic character. His success in each capacity sprang from his intense sympathy and his equally intense earnestness. Whatever with him was worth doing at all, was worth doing thoroughly. Anything he undertook, no matter what, he went in at, according to the good old sea phrase, with a will. He always endeavoured to accomplish whatever had to be accomplished as well as it could possibly be effected within the reach of his capabilities. Whether it were pastime or whether it were serious business, having once taken anything in hand, he applied to it the whole of his energies. Hence, as an amateur actor, he was simply unapproachable. He passed, in fact, beyond the range of mere amateurs, and was brought into contrast by right, with the most gifted professionals among his contemporaries. Hence, again, as an after-dinner speaker, he was nothing less than incomparable. "He spoke so well," Anthony Trollope has remarked, "that a public dinner became a blessing instead of a curse if he were in the chair—had its compensating twenty minutes of pleasure, even if he were called upon to propose a toast or thank the company for drinking his health." He did nothing by halves, but everything completely. How completely he gave himself up to the delivery of a speech or of a reading, Mr. Arthur Helps has summed up in less than a dozen words of singular emphasis. That keen observer has said, indeed quite truly, of Dickens,—"When he read or spoke, the whole man read or spoke." It was thus with him repeatedly, and always delightfully, in mere chance conversation. An incident related by him often became upon the instant a little acted drama. His mimetic powers were in many respects marvellous. In voice, in countenance, in carriage, almost, it might be said, at moments, in stature, he seemed to be a Proteus.

According to a curious account which has been happily preserved for us in the memoirs of the greatest reader of the last century, Henderson first of all exhibited his elocutionary skill by reciting (it was at Islington) an Ode on Shakspere. So exactly did he deliver this in Garrick's manner, that the acutest ear failed to distinguish the one from the other. One of those present declared, years afterwards, that he was certain the speaker *must be* either Garrick or Antichrist.

Imitative powers not one iota less extraordinary in their way were, at any moment, seemingly, at the command of the subject of this memorial. In one or two instances that might be named the assumption was all but identity. An aptitude of this particular kind, as everyone can appreciate upon the instant, would by necessity come wonderfully in aid of the illusive effect produced by readings that were in point of fact the mere vehicle or medium for a whole crowd of vivid impersonations. Anyone, moreover, possessing gifts like these, of a very peculiar description, not only naturally but inevitably enjoys himself every opportunity that may arise for displaying them to those about him, to his friends and intimates. "Man is of a companionable, conversing nature," says Goethe in his novel of The Renunciants, "his delight is great when he exercises faculties that have been given him, even though nothing further came of it." Seeing that something further readily did come of it in the instance of Charles Dickens, it can hardly be matter for surprise that the readings and impersonations which were first of all a home delight, should at length quite naturally have opened up before the popular author what was for him an entirely new, but at the same time a perfectly legitimate, career professionally.

Recitations or readings of his own works in public by a great writer are, in point of fact, as old as literature itself. They date back to the very origin of polite letters, both prose and poetic. It matters nothing whether there was one Homer, or whether there may have been a score of Homers, so far as the fact of oral publication applies to the Iliad and the Odyssey, nearly a thousand years (900) before the foundation of Christianity. By the lips of a single bard, or of a series of bards, otherwise of public declaimers or reciters, the world was first familiarised with the many enthralling tales strung together in those peerless masterpieces. Again, at a period of very nearly five hundred years (484) before the epoch of the Redemption, the Father of History came to lay the foundation, as it were, of the whole fabric of prose literature in a precisely similar manner—that is to say, by public readings or recitations. In point of fact, the instance there is more directly akin to the present argument. A musical cadence, or even possibly an instrumental accompaniment, may have marked the Homeric chant about Achilles and Ulysses. Whereas, obviously, in regard to Herodotus, the readings given by him at the Olympic games were readings in the modern sense, pure and simple. Lucian has related the incident, not only succinctly, but picturesquely.

Herodotus, then in his fiftieth year, reflected for a long while seriously how he might, with the least trouble and in the shortest time, win for himself and his writings a large amount of glory and reputation. Shrinking from the fatigue involved in the labour of visiting successively one after another the chief cities of the Athenians, the Corinthians, and the Lacedæmonians, he ingeniously hit upon the notion of appearing in person at the Olympian Games, and of there addressing himself simultaneously to the very pick and flower of the whole Greek population. Providing himself beforehand with the choicest portions or select passages from his great narrative, he there read or declaimed those fragments of his History to the assembled multitude from the stage or platform of the theatre. And he did this, moreover, with such an evident captivation about him, not only in the style of his composition, but in the very manner of its delivery, that the applause of his hearers interrupted him repeatedly—the close of these recitations by the great author-reader being greeted with prolonged and resounding acclamations. Nay, not only are these particulars related as to the First Reading recorded as having been given by a Great Author, but, further than that, there is the charming incident described of Thucydides, then a boy of fifteen, listening entranced among the audience to the heroic occurrences recounted by the sonorous and impassioned voice of the annalist, and at the climax of it all bursting into tears. Lucian's comment upon that earliest Reading might, with a change of names, be applied almost word for word to the very latest of these kinds of intellectual exhibitions. "None were ignorant," he says, "of the name of Herodotus; nor was there a single person in Greece who had not either seen him at the Olympics, or heard those speak of him that came from thence: so that in what place soever he came the inhabitants pointed with their finger, saying 'This is that Herodotus who has written the Persian Wars in the Ionic dialect, this is he who has celebrated our victories.' Thus the harvest which he reaped from his histories was, the receiving in one assembly the general applause of all Greece, and the sounding his fame, not only in one place and by a single trumpet, but by as many mouths as there had been spectators in that assembly." As recently as within these last two centuries, indeed, both in the development of the career of Molière and in the writing of his biography by Voltaire, the whole question as to the propriety of a great author becoming the public interpreter of his own imaginings has been, not only discussed, but defined with precision and in the end authoritatively proclaimed. Voltaire, in truth, has significantly remarked, in his "Vie de Molière," when referring to Poquelin's determination to become Comedian as well as Dramatist, that among the Athenians, as is perfectly well known, authors not only frequently performed in their own dramatic productions, but that none of them ever felt dishonoured by speaking gracefully in the presence and hearing of their fellow-citizens.* In arriving at this decision, however,

* "On sait que chez les Athéniens, les auteurs jouaient souvent dans

it will be remarked that one simple but important proviso or condition is indicated—not to be dishonoured they must speak with grace, that is, effectively. Whenever an author can do this, the fact is proclaimed by the public themselves. Does he lack the dramatic faculty, is he wanting in elocutionary skill, is his delivery dull, are his features inexpressive, is his manner tedious, are his readings marked only by their general tameness and mediocrity, be sure of this, he will speedily find himself talking only to empty benches, his enterprise will cease and determine, his name will no longer prove an attraction. Abortive adventures of this kind have in our own time been witnessed.

With Charles Dickens's Readings it was entirely different. Attracting to themselves at the outset, by the mere glamour of his name, enormous audiences, they not only maintained their original *prestige* during a long series of years—during an interval of fifteen years altogether—but the audiences brought together by them, instead of showing any signs of diminution, very appreciably, on the contrary, increased and multiplied. Crowds were turned away from the doors, who were unable to obtain admittance. The last reading of all collected together the largest audience that has ever been assembled, that ever can by possibility be assembled for purely reading purposes,

leurs pieces, et qu'ils n'etoient point déshonorés pour parler avec grace devant leurs concitoyens."

within the walls of St. James's Hall, Piccadilly. Densely packed from floor to ceiling, these audiences were habitually wont to hang in breathless expectation upon every inflection of the author-reader's voice, upon every glance of his eye,—the words he was about to speak being so thoroughly well remembered by the majority before their utterance that, often, the rippling of a smile over a thousand faces simultaneously anticipated the laughter which an instant afterwards greeted the words themselves when they were articulated.

Altogether, from first to last, there must have been considerably more than Four Hundred—very nearly, indeed, Five Hundred—of these Readings, each one among them in itself a memorable demonstration. Through their delightful agency, at the very outset, largess was scattered broadcast, abundantly, and with a wide open hand, among a great variety of recipients, whose interests, turn by turn, were thus exclusively subserved, at considerable labour to himself, during a period of several years, by this large-hearted entertainer.

Eventually the time arrived when it became necessary to decide, whether an exhausting and unremunerative task should be altogether abandoned, or whether readings hitherto given solely for the benefit of others, should be thenceforth adopted as a perfectly legitimate source of income for himself professionally.

The ball was at his feet: should it be rolled on, or fastidiously turned aside by reason of certain fantastic notions as to its derogating, in some inconceivable way, from the dignity of authorship? That was the alternative in regard to which Dickens had to decide, and upon which he at once, as became him, decided manfully. The ball was rolled on, and, as it rolled, grew in bulk like a snowball. It accumulated for him, as it advanced, and that too within a wonderfully brief interval, a very considerable fortune. It strengthened and extended his already widely-diffused and intensely personal popularity. By making him, thus, distinctly a Reader himself, it brought him face to face with vast multitudes of his own readers in the Old World and in the New, in all parts of the United Kingdom, and at last, upon the occasion of his second visit to America, an expedition adventured upon expressly to that end, in all parts of the United States.

And these Readings were throughout so conspicuously and so radiantly a success, that even in the recollection of them, now that they are things of the past, it may be said that they have already beneficially influenced, and are still perceptibly advancing, the wider and keener appreciation of the writings themselves. In its gyrations the ball then rolling at the Reader's foot imparted a momentum to one far nobler and more lasting—that of the Novelist's reputation, one that in its movement gives no sign of slackening—"labitur et labetur in omne volubilis ævum."

The long continuance of the remarkable success attendant upon the Readings all through, is only to be explained by the extraordinary care and earnestness the Reader lavished continuously upon his task when once it had been undertaken. In this he was only in another phase of his career, consistently true to the one simple rule adopted by him as an artist throughout. What that rule was anyone might see at a glance on turning over the leaves of one of his books, it matters not which, in the original manuscript. There, the countless alterations, erasures, interpolations, transpositions, interlineations, shew plainly enough the minute and conscientious thought devoted to the perfecting, so far as might be in any way possible, of the work of composition. What reads so unaffectedly and so felicitously, it is then seen, is but the result of exquisite consideration. It is Sheridan's whimsical line which declares that,—

> "Easy writing's cursed hard reading."

And it is Pope who summarizes the method by which not "easy writing" but "ease *in* writing" is arrived at, where it is said of those who have acquired a mastery of the craft,—

> "They polish all with so much life and ease,
> You think 'tis nature and a knack to please:
> But ease in writing flows from art, not chance;
> As those move easiest who have learn'd to dance."

Precisely the same elaboration of care, which all through his career was dedicated by Charles Dickens to the most delightful labour of his life, that of writing, was accorded by him to the lesser but still eminently intellectual toil of preparing his Readings for representation. It was not by any means that, having written a story years previously, he had, in his new capacity as a reciter, merely to select two or three chapters from it, and read them off with an air of animation. Virtually, the fragmentary portions thus taken from his larger works were re-written by him, with countless elisions and eliminations after having been selected. Reprinted in their new shape, each as "A Reading," they were then touched and re-touched by their author, pen in hand, until, at the end of a long succession of revisions, the pages came to be cobwebbed over with a wonderfully intricate network of blots and lines in the way of correction or of obliteration. Several of the leaves in this way, what with the black letter-press on the white paper, being scored out or interwoven with a tracery in red ink and blue ink alternately, present to view a curiously parti-coloured or tesselated appearance. As a specimen page, however, will afford a more vivid illustration upon the instant of what is referred to, than could be conveyed by any mere verbal description, a fac-simile is here introduced of a single page taken from the "Reading of Little Dombey."

Whatever thought was lavished thus upon the composition of the Readings, was lavished quite as unstintingly upon the manner of their delivery. Thoroughly natural, impulsive, and seemingly artless, though that manner always appeared at the moment, it is due to the Reader as an artist to assert that it was throughout the result of a scarcely credible amount of forethought and preparation. It is thus invariably indeed with every great proficient in the histrionic art, even with those who are quite erroneously supposed by the outer public to trust nearly everything to the momentary impulses of genius, and who are therefore presumed to disdain anything whatever in the way either of forethought or of actual preparation by rehearsal.

According to what is, even down to this present day, very generally conjectured, Edmund Kean, one of the greatest tragedians who ever trod the stage, is popularly imagined to have always played simply, as might be said, hap-hazard, trusting himself to the spur of the moment for throwing himself into a part passionately;—the fact being exactly the reverse in his regard, according to the earliest and most accurate of his biographers. Erratic, fitful though the genius of Edmund Kean unquestionably was—rendering him peerless as Othello, incomparable as Overreach—we are told in Mr. Procter's life of him, that "he studied long and anxiously," frequently until many hours after midnight.* No matter what his occupations previously might have been, or how profound his exhaustion through rehearsing in the forenoon, and performing in the evening, and sharing in convivialities afterwards, Barry Cornwall relates of him

* Barry Cornwall's Life of Edmund Kean, Vol. II. p. 85.

that he would often begin to study when his family had retired for the night, practising in solitude, after he had transformed his drawing-room into a stage in miniature. "Here," says his biographer, "with a dozen candles, some on the floor, some on the table, and some on the chimney-piece, and near the pier-glass, he would act scene after scene: considering the emphasis, the modulation of the verse, and the fluctuations of the character with the greatest care." And this, remember, has relation to one who was presumably about the most spontaneous and impulsive actor who ever flashed meteor-like across the boards of a theatre. Whoever has the soul of an artist grudges no labour given to his art, be he reader or actor, author or tragedian. Charles Dickens certainly spared none to his Readings in his conscientious endeavour to give his own imaginings visible and audible embodiment. The sincerity of his devotion to his task, when once it had been taken in hand, was in its way something remarkable.

Acting of all kinds has been pronounced by Mrs. Butler—herself in her own good day a rarely accomplished reader and a fine tragic actress—"a monstrous anomaly." * As illustrative of her meaning in which phrase, she then adds, "John Kemble and Mrs. Siddons were always in earnest in what they were about; Miss O'Neil used to cry bitterly in all her tragic parts; whilst Garrick could be making faces

* Fanny Kemble's Journal, Vol. II. p. 130.

and playing tricks in the middle of his finest points, and Kean would talk gibberish while the people were in an uproar of applause at his." Fanny Kemble further remarks: "In my own individual instance, I know that sometimes I could turn every word I am saying into burlesque,"—immediately observing here, in a reverential parenthesis "(never Shakspere, by-the-bye)—and at others my heart aches and I cry real, bitter, warm tears as earnestly as if I was in earnest." Reading which last sentence, one might very safely predicate that in the one instance, where she could turn her words into burlesque, she would be certain to act but indifferently, whereas in the other, with the hot, scalding tears running down her face, she could not by necessity do otherwise than act to admiration.

So thorough and consistent throughout his reading career was the sincerity of Dickens in his impersonations, that his words and looks, his thoughts and emotions were never mere make-believes, but always, so far as the most vigilant eye or the most sensitive ear could detect, had their full and original significance.

With all respect for Miss O'Neil's emotion, and for that candidly confessed to by Mrs. Butler, as having been occasionally evidenced by herself, the true art, we should have said, subsists in the indication and the repression, far rather than in the actual exhibition or manifestation of the emotions that are to be represented. Better by far than the familiar *si vis me flere* axiom of

Horace, who there tells us, "If you would have me weep, you must first weep yourself," is the sagacious comment on it in the *Tatler*, where (No. 68) the essayist remarks, with subtle discrimination: "The true art seems to be when you would have the person you represent pitied, you must show him at once, in the highest grief, and struggling to bear it with decency and patience. In this case," adds the writer, "we sigh for him, and give him every groan he suppresses." As for the extravagant idea of any artist, however great, identifying himself for the time being with the part he is enacting, who is there that can wonder at the snort of indignation with which Doctor Johnson, talking one day about acting, asked Mr. Kemble, "Are you, sir, one of those enthusiasts who believe yourself transformed into the very character you represent?" Kemble answering, according to Boswell, that he had never himself felt so strong a persuasion—"To be sure not, sir," says Johnson, "the thing is impossible." Adding, with one of his dryly comical extravagances: "And if Garrick really believed himself to be that monster Richard the Third, he deserved to be hanged every time he performed it." What Dickens himself really thought of these wilder affectations of intensity among impersonators, is, with delicious humour, plainly enough indicated through that preposterous reminiscence of Mr. Crummles, "We had a first-tragedy man in our company once, who, when he played Othello, used to black himself all over! But that's feeling a part, and going into it as if you meant it; it isn't usual—more's the pity." Thoroughly giving himself up to the representation of whatever character he was endeavouring at the moment to portray, or rather to impersonate, Charles Dickens so completely held his judgment the while in equipoise, as master of his two-fold craft—that is, both as creator and as elocutionist, as author and as reader—that, as an invariable rule, he betrayed neither of those signs of insincerity, by the inadvertent revelation of which all sense of illusion is utterly and instantly dissipated.

Whatever scenes he described, those scenes his hearers appeared to be actually witnessing themselves. He realised everything in his own mind so intensely, that listening to him we realised what he spoke of by sympathy. Insomuch that one might, in his own words, say of him, as David Copperfield says of Mr. Peggotty, when the latter has been recounting little Emily's wanderings: "He saw everything he related. It passed before him, as he spoke, so vividly, that, in the intensity of his earnestness, he presented what he described to me with greater distinctness than I can express. I can hardly believe—writing now long afterwards—but that I was actually present in those scenes; they are impressed upon me with such an astonishing air of fidelity." While, on the one hand, he never repeated the words that had to be delivered phlegmatically, or as by rote; on the other hand, he never permitted voice, look, gesture, to pass the limits of discretion, even at moments the most impassioned; as, for example, where Nancy, in the famous murder-scene, shrieked forth her last gasping and despairing appeals to her brutal paramour. The same thing may be remarked again in regard to all the more tenderly pathetic of his delineations. His tones then were often subdued almost to a whisper, every syllable, nevertheless, being so distinctly articulated as to be audible in the remotest part of a vast hall like that in Piccadilly.

Whatever may be insinuated in regard to those particular portions of the writings of our great novelist by cynical depreciators, who have not the heart to recognise—as did Lord Jeffrey, for instance, one of the keenest and shrewdest critics of his age—the exquisite pathos of a death-scene like that of little Nell or of little Paul Dombey, in the utterance by himself of those familiar passages nothing but the manliest emotion was visible and audible from first to last. Insomuch was this the case, that the least impressionable of his hearers might readily have echoed those noble words, written years ago, out of an overflowing heart, in regard to Charles Dickens, by his great rival and his intense admirer, W. M. Thackeray: "In those admirable touches of tender humour, who ever equalled this great genius? There are little words and phrases in his books which are like personal benefits to the reader. What a place to hold in the affections of men! What an awful responsibility hanging over a writer!" And so on. Thackeray saying all this! Thackeray speaking thus in ejaculatory sentences indicative of his gratitude and of his admiration! Passages that to men like William Thackeray and Francis Jeffrey were expressive only of inimitable tenderness, might be read dry-eyed by less keen appreciators, from the printed page, might even be ludicrously depreciated by them as mere mawkish sentimentality. But, even among these, there was hardly one who could hear those very passages read by Dickens himself without recognising at last, what had hitherto remained unperceived and unsuspected, the gracious and pathetic beauty animating every thought and every word in the original descriptions. Equally, it may be said, in the delineation of terror and of pathos, in the murder-scene from Oliver Twist, and in the death-scene of little Dombey, the novelist-reader attained success by the simple fact of his never once exaggerating.

It has been well remarked by an eminent authority upon the art of elocution, whose opinions have been already quoted in these pages, to wit, John Ireland, that "There is a point to which the passions must be raised to display that exhibition of them which scatters contagious tenderness through the whole theatre, but carried, though but the breadth of a hair, beyond that point, the picture becomes an overcharged caricature, as likely to create laughter as diffuse distress." Never, perhaps, has that subtle boundary-line been hit with more admirable dexterity, just within the hair's breadth here indicated, than it was, for example, in Macready's impersonation of Virginius, where his scream in the camp-scene betrayed his instantaneous appreciation of the wrong meditated by Appius Claudius against the virginal purity of his daughter. As adroitly, in his way, as that great master of his craft, who was for so many years among his most cherished friends and intimates, Dickens kept within the indicated lines of demarcation, beyond which no impersonator, whether upon the stage or upon the platform, can ever pass for a single instant with impunity.

Speaking of Munden, in one of the most charming of his Essays, Charles Lamb has said, "I have seen him diffuse a glow of sentiment which has made the pulse of a crowded house beat like that of one man; when he has come in aid of the pulpit, doing good to the moral heart of a people." The words, applied thus emphatically to the humorous and often grotesque comedian, are exactly applicable to Dickens as a Reader. And, as Elia remarks of Munden at another moment, "he is not one, but legion; not so much a comedian as a company"—any one might say identically the same of Dickens, who bears in remembrance the wonderful variety of his impersonations.

Attending his Readings, character after character appeared before us, living and breathing, in the flesh, as we looked and listened. It mattered nothing, just simply nothing, that the great author was there all the while before his audience in his own identity. His evening costume was a matter of no consideration—the flower in his button-hole, the paper-knife in his hand, the book before him, that earnest, animated, mobile, delightful face, that we all knew by heart through his ubiquitous photographs—all were equally of no account whatever. We knew that he alone was there all the time before us, reading, or, to speak more accurately, re-creating for us, one and all—while his lips were articulating the familiar words his hand had written so many years previously—the most renowned of the imaginary creatures peopling his books. Watching him, hearkening to him, while he stood there unmistakably before his audience, on the raised platform, in the glare of the gas-burners shining down upon him from behind the pendant screen immediately above his head, his individuality, so to express it, altogether disappeared, and we saw before us instead, just as the case might happen to be, Mr. Pickwick, or Mrs. Gamp, or Dr. Marigold, or little Paul Dombey, or Mr. Squeers, or Sam Weller, or Mr. Peggotty, or some other of those immortal personages. We were as conscious, as though we saw them, of the bald head, the spectacles, and the little gaiters of Mr. Pickwick—of the snuffy tones, the immense umbrella, and the voluminous bonnet and gown of Mrs. Gamp—of the belcher necktie, the mother-of-pearl buttons and the coloured waistcoat of the voluble Cheap Jack—of little Paul's sweet face and gentle accents—of the one eye and the well-known pair of Wellingtons, adorning the head and legs of Mr. Wackford Squeers—of Sam's imperturbable nonchalance—and of Mr. Peggotty's hearty, briny, sou'-wester of a voice and general demeanour!

Even the lesser characters—those which are introduced into the original works quite incidentally, occupying there a wholly subordinate position, filling up a space in the crowded tableaux, always in the background—were then at last brought to the fore in the course of these Readings, and suddenly and for the first time assumed to themselves a distinct importance and individuality. Take, for instance, the nameless lodging-housekeeper's slavey, who assists at Bob Sawyer's party, and who is described in the original work as "a dirty, slipshod girl, in black cotton stockings, who might have passed for the neglected daughter of a superannuated dustman in very reduced circumstances." No one had ever realised the crass stupidity of that remarkable young person—dense and impenetrable as a London fog—until her first introduction in these Readings, with "Please, Mister Sawyer, Missis Raddle wants to speak to *you!*"—the dull, dead-level of her voice ending in the last monosyllable with a series of inflections almost amounting to a chromatic passage. Mr. Justice Stareleigh, again! nobody had ever conceived the world of humorous suggestiveness underlying all the words put into his mouth until the author's utterance of them came to the readers of

Pickwick with the surprise of a revelation. Jack Hopkins in like manner—nobody, one might say, had ever dreamt of as he was in Dickens's inimitably droll impersonation of him, until the lights and shades of the finished picture were first of all brought out by the Reading. Jack Hopkins!—with the short, sharp, quick articulation, rather stiff in the neck, with a dryly comic look just under the eyelids, with a scarcely expressible relish of his own for every detail of that wonderful story of his about the "neckluss," an absolute and implicit reliance upon Mr. Pickwick's gullibility, and an inborn and ineradicable passion for chorusing.

As with the characters, so with the descriptions. One was life itself, the other was not simply word-painting, but realisation. There was the Great Storm at Yarmouth, for example, at the close of David Copperfield. Listening to that Reading, the very portents of the coming tempest came before us!—the flying clouds in wild and murky confusion, the moon apparently plunging headlong among them, "as if, in a dread disturbance of the laws of nature, she had lost her way and were frightened," the wind rising "with an extraordinary great sound," the sweeping gusts of rain coming before it "like showers of steel," and at last, down upon the shore and by the surf among the turmoil of the blinding wind, the flying stones and sand, "the tremendous sea itself," that came rolling in with an awful noise absolutely confounding to the beholder! In all fiction there is no grander description than that of one of the sublimest spectacles in nature. The merest fragments of it conjured up the entire scene—aided as those fragments were by the look, the tones, the whole manner of the Reader. The listener was there with him in imagination upon the beach, beside David. He was there, lashed and saturated with the salt spray, the briny taste of it on his lips, the roar and tumult in his ears—the height to which the breakers rose, and, looking over one another bore one another down and rolled in, in interminable hosts, becoming at last, as it is written in that wonderful chapter (55) of David Copperfield, "most appalling!" There, in truth, the success achieved was more than an elocutionary triumph—it was the realisation to his hearers, by one who had the soul of a poet, and the gifts of an orator, and the genius of a great and vividly imaginative author, of a convulsion of nature when nature bears an aspect the grandest and the most astounding. However much a masterly description, like that of the Great Storm at Yarmouth, may be admired henceforth by those who never had the opportunity of attending these Readings, one might surely say to them, as Æschines said to the Rhodians, when they were applauding the speech of his victorious rival: "How much greater would have been your admiration if only you could have heard him deliver it!"

THE READINGS
IN
ENGLAND AND AMERICA.

How it happened that Charles Dickens came to give any readings at all from his own writings has already, in the preceding pages, been explained. What is here intended to be done is to put on record, as simply and as accurately as possible, the facts relating to the labours gone through by the Novelist in his professional character as a Public Reader. It will be then seen, immediately those facts have come to be examined in their chronological order, that they were sufficiently remarkable in many respects, as an episode in the life of a great author, to justify their being chronicled in some way or other, if only as constituting in their aggregate a wholly unexampled incident in the history of literature.

No writer, it may be confidently asserted, has ever enjoyed a wider popularity during his own life-time than Charles Dickens; or rather it might be said more accurately, no writer has ever enjoyed *so* wide a popularity among his own immediate contemporaries. And it was a popularity in many ways exceptional.

It knew no fluctuation. It lasted without fading or faltering during thirty-four years altogether, that is to say, throughout the whole of Dickens's career as a novelist. It began with his very first book, when, as Thackeray put it, "the young man came and took his place calmly at the head of the whole tribe, as the master of all the English humorists of his generation." It showed no sign whatever of abatement, when, in the middle of writing his last book, the pen fell from his hand on that bright summer's day, and through his death a pang of grief was brought home to millions of English-speaking people in both hemispheres. For his popularity had, among other distinctive characteristics, certainly this,—it was so peculiarly personal a popularity, his name being endeared to the vast majority who read his books with nothing less than affectionate admiration.

Besides all this, it was his privilege throughout the whole of his literary career to address not one class, or two or three classes, but all classes of the reading public indiscriminately—the most highly educated and the least educated, young and old, rich and poor. His writings obtained the widest circulation, of course, among those who were the most numerous, such as among the middle classes and the better portion of the artisan population, but they found at the same time the keenest and cordialest appreciation among those who were necessarily the best qualified to pronounce an opinion upon their merits, among critics as gifted as Jeffrey and Sydney Smith, and among rivals as illustrious as Lytton and Thackeray. It seems appropriate, therefore, that we should be enabled to add now, in regard to the possession of this exceptional reputation, and of a popularity in itself so instant, sustained, personal, and comprehensive, that, thanks entirely to these Readings, he was brought into more intimate relations individually with a considerable portion at least of the vast circle of his own readers, than have ever been established between any other author who could be named and *his* readers, since literature became a profession.

Strictly speaking, the very first Reading given by Charles Dickens anywhere, even privately, was that which took place in the midst of a little home-group, assembled one evening in 1843, for the purpose of hearing the "Christmas Carol," prior to its publication, read by him in the Lincoln's-Inn Square Chambers of the intimate friend to whom, eighteen years afterwards, was inscribed, as "of right," the Library Edition of all the Novelist's works collectively. Thus unwittingly, and as it seems to us not unbefittingly, was rehearsed on the hearth of Dickens's future biographer, the first of the long series of Readings, afterwards to be given very publicly indeed, and to vast multitudes of people on both sides of the Atlantic.

As nearly as possible ten years after this, the public Readings commenced, and during the five next years were continued, though they were so but very intermittingly. Throughout that interval they were invariably given for the benefit of others, the proceeds of each Reading being applied to some generous purpose, the nature of which was previously announced. It was in the Town Hall at Birmingham, that immediately before the Christmas of 1853, the first of all these public Readings took place in the presence of an audience numbering fully two thousand. About a year before that, the Novelist had pledged himself to give this reading, or rather a series of three readings, for the purpose of increasing the funds of a new Literary and Scientific Institution then projected in Birmingham. On Thursday, the 6th of January, 1853, a silver-gilt salver and a diamond ring, accompanied by an address, expressive of the admiration of the subscribers to the testimonial, had been publicly presented in that town to the popular author, at the rooms of the Society of Arts in Temple Row. The kind of feeling inspiring this little incident may be recognised through the inscription on the salver, which intimated that it, "together with a diamond ring, was presented to Charles Dickens, Esq., by a number of his admirers in Birmingham, on the occasion of the literary and artistic banquet in that town, on the 6th of January, 1853, as a sincere testimony of their appreciation of his varied literary acquirements, and of the genial philosophy and high moral teaching which characterise his writings." It was upon the morrow of the banquet referred to in this inscription, a banquet which took place at Dee's Hotel immediately after the presentation of the testimonial to the Novelist, that the latter generously proposed to give later on some public Readings from his own books, in furtherance of the newly meditated Birmingham and Midland Institute.

The proposition, in fact, was thrown out, gracefully and almost apologetically, in a letter, addressed by him to Mr. Arthur Ryland on the following day, the 7th of January. In this singularly interesting communication, which was read by its recipient on the ensuing Monday, at a meeting convened in the theatre of the Philosophical Institution, not only did Charles Dickens offer to read his "Christmas Carol" some time during the course of the next Christmas, in the Town Hall at Birmingham, but referring to the complete novelty of his proposal, he thus plainly intimated that the occasion would constitute his very first appearance upon any public platform as a Reader, while explaining, at the same time, the precise nature of the suggested entertainment. "It would," he said, "take about two hours, with a pause of ten minutes half-way through. There would be some novelty in the thing, as *I have never done it in public*, though I have in private, and (if I may say so) with a great effect on the hearers." He further remarked, "I was so inexpressibly gratified last night by the warmth and enthusiasm of my Birmingham friends, that I feel half ashamed this morning of so poor an offer: but as I decided on making it to you before I came down yesterday, I propose it nevertheless." As a matter of course the proposition was gratefully accepted, the Novelist formally undertaking to give the proffered Readings in the ensuing Christmas. This promise, before the year was out, Dickens returned from abroad expressly to fulfil—hastening homeward to that end, after a brief autumnal excursion in Italy and Switzerland with two of his friends, the late Augustus Egg, R. A., and Wilkie Collins, the novelist. On the arrival of the three in Paris, they were there joined by Charles Dickens's eldest son, who, having passed through his course at Eton, had just then been completing his scholastic education at Leipsic. The party thus increased to a *partie carrée*, hastened homewards more hurriedly than would otherwise have been necessary, so as to enable the author punctually to fulfil his long-standing engagement.

It was on Tuesday, the 27th of December, 1853, therefore, that the very first of these famous Readings came off in the Town Hall at Birmingham. The weather was wretched, but the hall was crowded, and the audience enthusiastic. The Reading, which was the "Christmas Carol," extended over more than three hours altogether, showing how very little of the original story the then unpractised hand of the Reader had as yet eliminated. Notwithstanding the length of the entertainment, the unflagging interest, more even than the hearty and reiterated applause of those who were assembled, showed the lively sense the author's first audience had of his newly-revealed powers as a narrator and impersonator. On the next day but one, Thursday, the 29th of December, he read there, to an equally large concourse, the "Cricket on the Hearth." Upon the following evening, Friday, the 30th of December, he repeated the "Carol" to another densely packed throng of listeners, mainly composed, this time, according to his own express stipulation, of workpeople. So delighted were these unsophisticated hearers with their entertainer—himself so long familiarly known to them, but then for the first time seen and heard—that, at the end of the Reading, they greeted him with repeated rounds of cheering.

Those three Readings at Birmingham added considerably to the funds of the Institute, enhancing them at least to the extent of £400 sterling. In recognition of the good service thus effectively and delightfully rendered to a local institution, to the presidency of which Charles Dickens himself was unanimously elected, an exquisitely designed silver flower-basket was afterwards presented to the novelist's wife. This graceful souvenir had engraved upon it the following inscription: "Presented to Mrs. Charles Dickens by the Committee of the Birmingham and Midland Institute, as a slight acknowledgment of the debt of gratitude due to her husband, for his generous liberality in reading the 'Christmas Carol,' and the

'Cricket on the Hearth,' to nearly six thousand persons, in the Town Hall, Birmingham, on the nights of December 27, 29, and 30, 1853, in aid of the funds for the establishment of the Institute." The incident of these three highly successful Readings entailed upon the Reader, as events proved, an enormous amount of toil, none of which, however, did he ever grudge, in affording the like good service to others, at uncertain intervals, in all parts, sometimes the remotest parts, of the United Kingdom.

It would be beside our present purpose to catalogue, one after another, the various Readings given in this way by the Novelist, before he was driven to the necessity at last of either giving up reading altogether, or coming to the determination to adopt it, as he then himself expressed it, as one of his recognised occupations; that is, by becoming a Reader professionally. It is with his career in his professional capacity as a Reader that we have here to do. Until he had formally and avowedly assumed that position, his labours in this way were, as a matter of course, in no respect whatever systematised. They were uncertain, and in one sense, as the sequel shewed, purely tentative or preliminary. They yielded a world of delight, however, and did a world of good at the same time; while they were, unconsciously to himself, preparing the way effectually—that is, by ripening his powers and perfecting his skill through practice—for the opening up to himself, quite legitimately, of a new phase in his career as a man of letters. Previously, again and again, with the pen in his hand, he had proved himself to be the master-humorist of his time. He was now vividly to attest that fact by word of mouth, by the glance of his eye, by the application to the reading of his own books, of his exceptional mimetic and histrionic gifts as an elocutionist. Added to all this, by merely observing how readily he could pour, through the proceeds of these purely benevolent Readings, princely largess into the coffers of charities or of institutions in which he happened to be interested, he was to realise, what must otherwise have remained for him wholly unsuspected, that he had, so to speak, but to stretch forth his hand to grasp a fortune.

During the lapse of five years all this was at first very gradually, but at last quite irresistibly, brought home to his conviction. A few of the Readings thus given by him, out of motives of kindliness or generosity, may here, in passing, be particularised.

A considerable time after the three Readings just mentioned, and which were distinctly inaugurative of the whole of our author's reading career, there was one, which came off in Peterborough, that has not only been erroneously described as antecedent to those three Readings at Birmingham, but has been depicted, at the same time, with details in the account of it of the most preposterous character. The Reader, for example, has been portrayed,—in this purely apocryphal description of what throughout it is always referred to as though it were the first Reading of all, which it certainly was not,—as in a highly nervous state from the commencement of it to its conclusion! This being said of one who, when asked if he ever felt nervous while speaking in public, is known to have replied, "Not in the least"—adding, that "when first he took the chair he felt as much confidence as though he had already done the like a hundred times!" As corroborative of which remark, the present writer recalls to recollection very clearly the fact of Dickens saying to him one day,—saying it with a most whimsical air by-the-bye, but very earnestly,—"Once, and but once only in my life, I was—frightened!" The occasion he referred to was simply this, as he immediately went on to explain, that somewhere about the middle of the serial publication of David Copperfield, happening to be out of writing-paper, he sallied forth one morning to get a fresh supply at the stationer's. He was living then in his favourite haunt, at Fort House, in Broadstairs. As he was about to enter the stationer's shop, with the intention of buying the needful writing-paper, for the purpose of returning home with it, and at once setting to work upon his next number, not one word of which was yet written, he stood aside for a moment at the threshold to allow a lady to pass in before him. He then went on to relate—with a vivid sense still upon him of mingled enjoyment and dismay in the mere recollection—how the next instant he had overheard this strange lady asking the person behind the counter for the new green number. When it was handed to her, "Oh, this," said she, "I have read. I want the next one." The next one she was thereupon told would be out by the end of the month. "Listening to this, unrecognised," he added, in conclusion, "knowing the purpose for which I was there, and remembering that not one word of the number she was asking for was yet written, for the first and only time in my life, I felt—frightened!" So much for the circumstantial account put forth of this Reading at Peterborough, and of the purely imaginary nervousness displayed by the Reader, who, on the contrary, there, as elsewhere, was throughout perfectly self-possessed.

On Saturday, the 22nd December, 1855, in the Mechanics' Hall at Sheffield, another of these Readings was given, it being the "Carol," as usual, and the proceeds being in aid of the funds of that institution. The Mayor of Sheffield, who presided upon the occasion, at the close of the proceedings, presented to the author, as a suitable testimonial from a number of his admirers in that locality, a complete set of table cutlery.

An occasional Reading, moreover, was given at Chatham, to assist in defraying the expenses of the Chatham, Rochester, Strood, and Brompton Mechanics' Institution, of which the master of Gadshill was for thirteen years the President. His titular or official connection with this institute, in effect, was that of Perpetual President. His interest in it in that character ceased only with his life. Throughout the whole of the thirteen years during which he presided over its fortunes, he was in every imaginable way its most effective and energetic supporter. Six Readings in all were given by him at the Chatham Mechanics' Institution, in aid of its funds. The first, which was the "Christmas Carol," took place on the 27th December, 1857, the new Lecture Hall, which was appropriately decorated with evergreens and brilliantly illuminated, being crowded with auditors, conspicuous among whom were the officers of the neighbouring garrison and dockyard. The second, which consisted of "Little Dombey" and "The Trial Scene from Pickwick," came off on the 29th December, 1858. Long before any arrangement had been definitively made in regard to this second Reading, the local newspaper, in an apparently authoritative paragraph, announced, "on the best authority," that another Reading was immediately to be given, by Mr. Dickens, in behalf of the Mechanics' Institution. It is characteristic of him that he, thereupon, wrote to the Chatham newspaper, "I know nothing of your 'best authority,' except that he is (as he always is) preposterously and monstrously wrong." Eventually this Reading was arranged for, nevertheless, and came off at the date already mentioned. A third Reading at Chatham, comprising within it "The Poor Traveller" (the opening of which had a peculiar local interest), "Boots at the Holly Tree Inn," and "Mrs. Gamp," took place in 1860, on the 18th December. A fourth was given there on the 16th January, 1862, when the Novelist read his six selected chapters from "David Copperfield." A fifth, consisting of "Nicholas Nickleby at Dotheboys Hall," and "Mr. Bob Sawyer's Party," took place in 1863, on the 15th December. Finally, there came off the sixth of these Chatham readings, on the 19th December, 1865, when the "Carol" was repeated, with the addition of the great case of "Bardell *versus* Pickwick." Upwards of £400 were thus, as the fruit of these exhilarating entertainments, poured into the coffers of the Chatham Institute. It can hardly be wondered at that, in the annual reports issued by the committee, emphatic expression should have been more than once given to the deep sense of gratitude entertained by them for the services rendered to the institution by its illustrious president. A fragmentary portion of that issued by the committee in the January of 1864—referring, as it does, to Charles Dickens, in association with his home and his favourite haunts down at Gadshill—we are here tempted to give, as indicative of the feelings of pride and admiration with which the great author was regarded by his own immediate neighbours. After referring to the large sums realised for the institution through the Readings thus generously given by its president, the committee went on to say in this report, at the beginning of 1864, "Simply to have the name of one whose writings have become household words at every home and hearth where the English language is spoken, associated with their efforts for the public entertainment and improvement, must be considered a great honour and advantage. But, when to this is added the large pecuniary assistance derived from such a connection, your committee find that they—and, of course, the members whom they represent—owe a debt of gratitude to Mr. Dickens, which words can but poorly express. They trust that the home which he now occupies in the midst of the beautiful woodlands of Kent, and so near to the scene of his boyish memories and associations, may long be to him one of happiness and prosperity. If Shakspere, our greatest national poet, had before made Gadshill a classic spot, surely it is now doubly consecrated by genius since Dickens, the greatest and most genial of modern humorists, as well as one of the most powerful and pathetic delineators of human character, has fixed his residence there. To those who have so often and so lately been moved to laughter and tears by the humour and pathos of the inimitable writer and reader, and who have profited by his gratuitous services to the institution, your committee feel that they need make no apology for dwelling at some length upon this most agreeable part of their report." Thus profound were the feelings of respect, affection, and admiration with which the master-humorist was regarded by those who lived, and who were proud of living, in his own immediate neighbourhood.

On the evening of Tuesday, the 30th June, 1857, Charles Dickens read for the first time in London, at the then St. Martin's Hall, now the Queen's Theatre, in Long Acre. The occasion was one, in many respects, of peculiar interest. As recently as on the 8th of that month, Douglas Jerrold had breathed his last, quite unexpectedly. Dying in the fulness of his powers, and at little more than fifty years of age, he had passed away, it was felt, prematurely. As a tribute of affection to his memory, and of sympathy towards his widow and orphan children, those among his brother authors who had been more intimately associated with him in his literary career, organised, in the interests of his bereaved family, a series of entertainments. And in the ordering of the programme it was so arranged that this earliest metropolitan reading of one of his smaller works by Charles Dickens should be the second of these entertainments. Densely crowded in every part, St. Martin's Hall upon this occasion was the scene of as remarkable a reception and of as brilliant a success as was in any way possible. It was a wonderful success financially. As an elocutionary—or, rather, as a dramatic—display, it was looked forward to with the liveliest curiosity. The author's welcome when he appeared upon the platform was of itself a striking attestation of his popularity.

Upwards of fourteen years have elapsed since the occasion referred to, yet we have still as vividly in our remembrance, as though it were but an incident of yesterday, the enthusiasm of the reception then accorded to the great novelist by an audience composed, for the most part, of representative Londoners. The applause with which he was greeted, immediately upon his entrance, was so earnestly prolonged and sustained, that it threatened to postpone the Reading indefinitely. Silence having at last been restored, however, the Reader's voice became audible in the utterance of these few and simple words, by way of preliminary :—
"Ladies and gentlemen, I have the honour to read
"to you 'A Christmas Carol,' in four staves. Stave
"one, 'Marley's Ghost.'" The effect, by the way, becoming upon the instant rather incongruous, as the writer of this very well remembers, when, through a sudden and jarring recollection of what the occasion was that had brought us all together, the Reader began, with a serio-comic inflection, "Marley was dead : to begin with. There's no doubt whatever about that. The register of his burial was signed." And so on through those familiar introductory sentences, in which Jacob Marley's demise is insisted upon with such ludicrous particularity. The momentary sense of incongruity here referred to was lost, however, directly afterwards, as everyone's attention became absorbed in the author's own relation to us of his world-famous ghost-story of Christmas.

Whereas the First Reading of the tale down in the provinces had occupied three hours in its delivery, the First Reading of it in the metropolis had been diminished by half an hour. Beginning at 8 P. M., and ending at very nearly 10.30 P. M., with merely five minutes' interruption about midway, the entertainment so enthralled and delighted the audience throughout, that its close, after two hours and a half of the keenest attention, was the signal for a long outburst of cheers, mingled with the waving of hats and handkerchiefs. The description of the scene there witnessed is in no way exaggerated. It is the record of our own remembrance.

And the enthusiasm thus awakened among Charles Dickens's first London audience can hardly be wondered at, when we recall to mind Thackeray's expression of opinion in regard to that very same story of the Christmas Carol immediately after its publication, when he wrote in *Fraser*, July, 1844, under his pseudonym of M. A. Titmarsh: "It seems to me a national benefit, and to every man and woman who reads it a personal kindness;" adding, "The last two people I heard speak of it were women; neither knew the other, or the author, and both said, by way of criticism, 'God bless him!'" Precisely in the same way, it may here be said, in regard to that first night of his own public reading of it in St. Martin's Hall, that there was a genial grasp of the hand in the look of every kind face then turned towards the platform, and a "God bless him" in every one of the ringing cheers that accompanied his departure.

A Reading of the "Carol" was given by its author in the following December down at Coventry, in aid of the funds of the local institute. And about a twelvemonth afterwards, on the 4th of December, 1858, in grateful acknowledgment of what was regarded in those cases always as a double benefaction (meaning the Reading itself and its golden proceeds), the novelist was entertained at a public banquet, at the Castle Hotel, Coventry, when a gold watch was presented to him as a testimonial of admiration from the leading inhabitants.

Finally, as the last of all these non-professional readings by our author, there was given on Friday the 26th of March, 1858, a reading of the "Christmas Carol," in the Music Hall at Edinburgh. His audience consisted of the members of, or subscribers to, the Philosophical Institution. At the close of the evening the Lord Provost, who had been presiding, presented to the Reader a massive and ornate silver wassail bowl. Seventeen years prior to that, Charles Dickens had been publicly entertained in Edinburgh,—Professor Wilson having been the chairman of the banquet given then in his honour. He had been at that time enrolled a burgess and guildbrother of the ancient corporation of the metropolis of Scotland. He had, among other incidents of a striking character marking his reception there at the same period, seen, on his chance entrance into the theatre, the whole audience rise spontaneously in recognition of him, the musicians in the orchestra, with a courtly felicity, striking up the cavalier air of "Charley is my Darling." If only out of a gracious remembrance of all this, it seemed not inappropriate that the very last of the complimentary readings should have been given by the novelist at Edinburgh, and that the Lord Provost of Edinburgh should, as if by way of stirrup-cup, have handed to the Writer and Reader of the "Carol," that souvenir from its citizens, in honour of the author himself and of his favourite theme, Christmas.

It was in connection with the organisation of the series of entertainments, arranged during the summer of 1857, in memory of Jerrold, and in the interests of Jerrold's family, that the attention of Charles Dickens was first of all awakened to a recognition of the possibility that he might, with good reason, do something better than carry out his original intention, that, namely, of dropping these Readings altogether, as simply exhausting and unremunerative. He had long since come to realise that it could in no conceivable way whatever derogate from the dignity of his position as an author, to appear thus in various parts of the United Kingdom, before large masses of his fellow-countrymen, in the capacity of a Public Reader. His so appearing was a gratification to himself as an artist, and was clearly enough also a gratification to his hearers, as appreciators of his twofold art, both as Author and as Reader. He perceived clearly enough, therefore, that his labours in those associated capacities were perfectly compatible; that, in other words, he might, if he so pleased, quite reasonably accept the duties devolving upon him as a Reader, as among his legitimate avocations.

Conspicuous among those who had shared in the getting up of the Jerrold entertainments—including among them, as we have seen, the first of his own Readings in London—the novelist had especially observed the remarkable skill or aptitude, as a general organiser, manifested from first to last by the Honorary Secretary, into whose hands, in point of fact, had fallen the responsibility of the entire management. This Honorary Secretary was no other than Albert Smith's brother Arthur—one who was not only the right-hand, as it were, of the Ascender of Mont Blanc, and of the Traveller in China, but who (behind the scenes, and unknown to the public) was the veritable wire-puller, prompter, Figaro, factotum of that *farçeur* among story-tellers, and of that laughter-moving patterer among public entertainers. Arthur Smith, full of resource, of contrivance, and of readiness, possessed in fact all the qualifications essential to a rapid organiser. He was, of all men who could possibly have been hit upon, precisely the very one to undertake in regard to an elaborate enterprise, like that of a long series of Readings in the metropolis, and of a comprehensive tour of Readings in the provinces, the responsible duties of its commercial management. Brought together accidentally at the time of the Jerrold testimonial, the Honorary Secretary of the fund and the Author-reader of the "Carol" came, as it seems now, quite naturally, to be afterwards intimately associated with one another, more in connection with the scheme of professional Readings, which reasonably grew up at last out of the previous five years' Readings, of a purely complimentary character.

Altogether, as has been said on an earlier page, Charles Dickens cannot have given less than some Five Hundred Readings. As a professional Reader alone he gave considerably over Four Hundred. Beginning in the spring of 1858, and ending in the spring of 1870, his career in that capacity extended at intervals over a lapse of twelve years: those twelve years embracing within them several distinct tours in England, Ireland, and Scotland, and in the United States; and many either entirely distinct or carefully interwoven series in London at St. Martin's Hall, at the Hanover Square Rooms, and at St. James's Hall, Piccadilly.

The first series in the metropolis, and the first tour in the United Kingdom, were made in 1858, under Mr. Arthur Smith's management. The second provincial tour, partly in 1861, partly in 1862, and two sets of readings in London, one at the St. James's Hall in 1862, the other at the Hanover Square Rooms in 1863, took place under Mr. Thomas Headland's management. As many as four distinct, and all of them important tours, notably one on the other side of the Atlantic, were carried out between 1866 and 1869, both years inclusive, under Mr. George Dolby's management. As showing at once the proportion of the enormous aggregate of 423 Readings, with which these three managers were concerned, it may be added here that while the first-mentioned had to do with 111, and the second with 70, the third and last-mentioned had to do with as many as 242 altogether.

It was on the evening of Thursday, the 29th of April, 1858, that Charles Dickens first made his appearance upon a platform in a strictly professional character as a public Reader. Although, hitherto, he had never once read for himself, he did so then avowedly—not merely by printed announcement beforehand, but on addressing himself by word of mouth to the immense audience assembled there in St. Martin's Hall. The Reading selected for the occasion was "The Cricket on the Hearth," but before its commencement, the author spoke as follows, doing so with well remembered clearness of articulation, as though he were particularly desirous that every word should be thoroughly weighed by his hearers, and taken to heart, by reason of their distinctly explaining the relations in which he and they would thenceforth stand towards each other :—

"LADIES AND GENTLEMEN,—It may, perhaps, be

"known to you that, for a few years past I have been "accustomed occasionally to read some of my shorter "books to various audiences, in aid of a variety of "good objects, and at some charge to myself both in "time and money. It having at length become im-"possible in any reason to comply with these always "accumulating demands, I have had definitely to "choose between now and then reading on my own "account as one of my recognised occupations, or not "reading at all. I have had little or no difficulty in "deciding on the former course.

"The reasons that have led me to it—besides the "consideration that it necessitates no departure what-"ever from the chosen pursuits of my life—are three-"fold. Firstly, I have satisfied myself that it can "involve no possible compromise of the credit and "independence of literature. Secondly, I have long "held the opinion, and have long acted on the opinion, "that in these times whatever brings a public man "and his public face to face, on terms of mutual con-"fidence and respect, is a good thing. Thirdly, I "have had a pretty large experience of the interest "my hearers are so generous as to take in these occa-"sions, and of the delight they give to me, as a tried "means of strengthening those relations, I may "almost say of personal friendship, which it is my "great privilege and pride, as it is my great respon-"sibility, to hold with a multitude of persons who will "never hear my voice, or see my face.

"Thus it is that I come, quite naturally, to be here "among you at this time. And thus it is that I pro-"ceed to read this little book, quite as composedly as "I might proceed to write it, or to publish it in any "other way."

Remembering perfectly well, as we do, the precision with which he uttered every syllable of this little address, and the unmistakable cordiality with which its close was greeted, we can assert with confidence that Reader and Audience from the very first instant stood towards each other on terms of mutually respectful consideration. Remembering perfectly well, as we do, moreover, the emotion with which his last words were articulated and listened to on the occasion of his very last or Farewell Reading in the great hall near Piccadilly—and more than two thousand others must still perfectly well remember that likewise—we may no less confidently assert that those feelings had known no abatement, but on the contrary had, during the lapse of many delightful years, come to be not only confirmed but intensified.

Sixteen Readings were comprised in that first series in London, at St. Martin's Hall. Inaugurated, as we have seen, on the 29th of April, 1858, the series was completed on the 22nd of the ensuing July. It may here be interesting to mention that, midway in the course of these Sixteen Readings, he gave for the first time in London, on Thursday the 10th of June, "The Story of Little Dombey," and on the following Thursday, the 17th of June, also for the first time in London, "The Poor Traveller," "Boots at the Holly Tree Inn," and "Mrs. Gamp." Whatever the subject of the Reading, whatever the state of the weather, the hall was crowded in every part, from the stalls to the galleries. Eleven days after the London season closed, the Reader and his business manager began their enormous round of the provinces.

As many as Eighty-Seven Readings were given in the course of this one provincial excursion. The first took place on Monday, the 2nd of August, at Clifton; the last on Saturday, the 13th of November, at Brighton. The places visited in Ireland included Dublin and Belfast, Cork and Limerick. Those traversed in Scotland comprised Edinburgh and Dundee, Aberdeen, Perth, and Glasgow. As for England, besides the towns already named, others of the first importance were taken in quick succession, an extraordinary amount of rapid railway travelling being involved in the punctual carrying out of the prescribed programme. However different in their general character the localities might be, the Readings somehow appeared to have some especial attraction for each, whether they were given in great manufacturing towns, like Manchester or Birmingham; in fashionable watering-places, like Leamington or Scarborough; in busy outports, like Liverpool or Southampton; in ancient cathedral towns, like York or Durham, or in seaports as removed from each other, as Plymouth and Portsmouth. Localities as widely separated as Exeter from Harrogate, as Oxford from Halifax, or as Worcester from Sunderland, were visited, turn by turn, at the particular time appointed. In a comprehensive round, embracing within it Wakefield and Shrewsbury, Nottingham and Leicester, Derby and Huddersfield, the principal great towns were taken one after another. At Hull and Leeds, no less than at Chester and Bradford, as large and enthusiastic audiences were gathered together as, in their appointed times also were attracted to the Readings, in places as entirely dissimilar as Newcastle and Darlington, or as Sheffield and Wolverhampton.

The enterprise was, in its way, wholly unexampled. It extended over a period of more than three months altogether. It brought the popular author for the first time face to face with a multitude of his readers in various parts of the three kingdoms. And at every place, without exception throughout the tour, the adventure was more than justified, as a source of artistic gratification alike to himself and to his hearers, no less than as a purely commercial undertaking, the project throughout proving successful far beyond the most sanguine anticipations. Though the strain upon his energies, there can be no doubt of it, was very considerable, the Reader had brought vividly before him in recompense, on Eighty-Seven distinct occasions, the most startling proofs of his popularity—the financial results, besides this, when all was over, yielding substantial evidence of his having, indeed, won "golden opinions" from all sorts of people.

His provincial tour, it has been seen, closed at Brighton on the 13th of November. Immediately after this, it was announced that three Christmas Readings would be given in London at St. Martin's Hall—the first and second on the Christmas Eve and the Boxing Day of 1858, those being respectively Friday and Monday, and the third on Twelfth Night, Thursday, the 6th of January, 1859. Upon each of these occasions the "Christmas Carol" and the "Trial from Pickwick," were given to audiences that were literally overflowing, crowds of applicants each evening failing to obtain admittance. In consequence of this, three other Readings were announced for Thursday, the 13th, for Thursday, the 20th, and for Friday, the 28th of January—the "Carol" and "Trial" being fixed for the last time on the 13th; the Reading on the second of these three supplementary nights being "Little Dombey" and the "Trial from Pickwick;" the last of the three including within it, besides the "Trial," "Mrs. Gamp" and the "Poor Traveller." As affording conclusive proof of the sustained success of the Readings as a popular entertainment, it may here be added that advertisements appeared on the morrow of the one last mentioned, to the effect that "it has been found unavoidable to appoint two more Readings of the 'Christmas Carol' and the 'Trial from Pickwick'"—those two, by the way, being, from first to last, the most attractive of all the Readings. On Thursday, the 3rd, and on Tuesday, the 8th of February, the two last of these supplementary Readings in London, the aggregate of which had thus been extended from Three to Eight, were duly delivered. And in this way were completed the 111 Readings already referred to as having been given under Mr. Arthur Smith's management.

Upwards of two years and a half then elapsed without any more of the Readings being undertaken, either in the provinces or in the metropolis. During 1860, in fact, Great Expectations was appearing from week to week in *All the Year Round.* And it was a judicious rule with our author—broken only at the last, and fatally, at the very end of his twofold career as Writer and as Reader—never to give a series of Readings while one of his serial stories was being produced. At length, however, in the late summer, or early autumn of 1861, the novelist was sufficiently free from literary pre-occupations for another tour, and another series of Readings in London to be projected. The arrangements for each were sketched out by Mr. Arthur Smith, as the one still entrusted with the financial management of the undertaking. His health, however, was so broken by that time, that it soon became apparent that he could not reasonably hope to superintend in person the carrying out of the new enterprise. It was decided, therefore, provisionally, that Mr. Headland, who, upon the former occasion, had acted with him, should now, under his direction and as his representative, undertake the actual management. Before the projected tour of 1861 actually commenced, however, Mr. Arthur Smith had died, in September. The simply provisional arrangement lapsed in consequence, and upon Mr. Headland himself devolved the responsibility of carrying out the plans sketched out by his predecessor.

Although about the same time that had been allotted to the First Tour, namely a whole quarter, had been set apart for the Second, the latter included within it but very little more than half the number of Readings given in the earlier and more rapid round of the provinces. The Second Tour, in point of fact—beginning on Monday, the 28th of October, 1861, at Norwich, and terminating on Thursday, the 30th of January, 1862, at Chester—comprised within it Forty-Seven, instead of, as on the former occasion, Eighty-Seven readings altogether. Many of the principal towns and cities of England, not visited during the more comprehensive sweep made in 1858, through the three kingdoms, were now reached—the tour, this time, being restricted within the English boundaries. Lancaster and Carlisle, for example, Hastings and Canterbury, Ipswich and Colchester, were severally included in the new programme. Resorts of fashion, like Torquay and Cheltenham, were no longer overlooked. Preston in the north, Dover in the south, were each in turn the scene of a Reading. Bury St. Edmund's, in 1861, was reached on the 30th of October, and on the 25th of November an excursion was even made to the far-off border town of Berwick-upon-Tweed. Less hurried and less laborious than the first, this second tour was completed, as we have said, at Chester, just before the close of the first month of 1862, namely, on the 30th of January.

Then came the turn once more of London, where a series of Ten Readings was given in the St. James's Hall, Piccadilly. These ten Readings, beginning on Thursday, the 13th of March, were distributed over sixteen weeks, ending on Friday, the 27th of June. Another metropolitan series, still under Mr. Headland's management, was given as nearly as possible at the same period of the London season in the following twelvemonth. The Hanover Square Rooms were the scene of these Readings of 1863, which began on Monday, the 2nd of March, and ended on Saturday, the 13th of June, numbering in all not ten, as upon the last occasion, but Thirteen.

During the winter of this year, Two notable Readings were given by the Novelist at the British Embassy, in Paris, their proceeds being devoted to the British Charitable Fund in that capital. These Readings were so brilliantly successful, that, by particular desire, they were, a little time afterwards, supplemented by a Third, which was quite as numerously attended as either of its predecessors. The audience upon each occasion, partly English, partly French, comprised among their number many of the most gifted and distinguished of the Parisians. These three entertainments were given under the immediate auspices of the Earl Cowley, then Her Majesty's ambassador to the court of Napoleon III.

A considerable interval now elapsed, extending in fact over nearly three years altogether, before the author again appeared upon the platform in his capacity as a Reader, either in London or in the Provinces. During his last provincial tour, there had been some confusion caused to the general arrangements by reason of the abrupt but unavoidable postponement of a whole week's Readings, previously announced as coming off, three of them at Liverpool, one at Chester, and two at Manchester. These six readings instead, however, of duly taking place, as originally arranged, between the 16th and the 21st of December, 1861, had to be given four weeks later on, between the 13th and the 30th of the following January. The disarrangement of the programme thus caused arose simply from the circumstance of the wholly unlooked-for and lamented death of H.R.H. the Prince Consort. Another confusion in the carefully prepared plans for one of the London series, again, had been caused by an unexpected difficulty, at the last moment, in securing the great Hall in Piccadilly, that having been previously engaged on the required evenings for a series of musical entertainments. Hence the selection for that season of the

Hanover Square Rooms, which, at any rate for the West-end public, could not but be preferable to that earliest scene of the London Readings, St. Martin's Hall, Long Acre. Apart from every other consideration, however, the Novelist's remembrance of the confusions and disarrangements which had been incidental to his last provincial tour, and to the last series of his London Readings, rather disinclined him to hasten the date of his re-appearance in his character as a public Reader. As it happened, besides, after the summer of 1863, nearly two years elapsed, between the May of 1864 and the November of 1865, during which he was in a manner precluded from seriously entertaining any such project by the circumstance that the green numbers of "Our Mutual Friend" were, all that while, in course of publication. Even when that last of his longer serial stories had been completed, it is doubtful whether he would have cared to take upon himself anew the irksome stress and responsibility inseparable from one of those doubly laborious undertakings—a lengthened series of Readings in London, coupled with, or rather interwoven with, another extended tour through the provinces.

As it fortunately happened, however, very soon after the completion of "Our Mutual Friend," Charles Dickens had held out to him a double inducement to undertake once more the duties devolving upon him in his capacity as a Reader. The toil inseparable from the Readings themselves, as well as the fatigue resulting inevitably from so much rapid travelling hither and thither by railway during the period set apart for their delivery, would still be his. But at the least, according to the proposition now made to him, the Reader would be relieved from further care as to the general supervision, and at any rate, from all sense of responsibility in the revived project as a purely financial or speculative undertaking. The Messrs. Chappell, of New Bond Street, a firm skilled in the organizing of public entertainments of various kinds, chiefly if not exclusively until then, entertainments of a musical character, offered, in fact, in 1866 to assume to themselves thenceforth the whole financial responsibility of the Readings in the Metropolis and throughout the United Kingdom. According to the proposal originally submitted to the Novelist by the Messrs. Chappell, and at once frankly accepted by him, a splendid sum was guaranteed to him in remuneration. Twice afterwards those terms were considerably increased,—and upon each occasion, it should be added, quite spontaneously.

Another inducement was held out to the Reader besides that of his being relieved from all further sense of responsibility in the undertaking as a merely speculative enterprise. It related to the chance of his finding himself released also from any further sense of solicitude as to the conduct of the general business management. The inducement, here, however, was of course in no way instantly recognizable. Experience alone could show the fitness for his post of the Messrs. Chappell's representative. As good fortune would have it, nevertheless, here precisely was an instance in which Mr. Layard's famous phrase about the right man in the right place, was directly applicable. As a thoroughly competent business manager, and as one whose companionship of itself had a heartening influence in the midst of enormous toil, Mr. Dolby speedily came to be recognised as the very man for the position, as the very one who in all essential respects it was most desirable should have been selected.

A series of Thirty Readings was at once planned under his supervision. It consisted for the first time of a tour through England and Scotland, interspersed with Readings every now and then in the Metropolis. The Reader's course in this way seemed to be erratic, but the whole scheme was admirably well arranged beforehand, and once entered upon, was carried out with the precision of clockwork. .These thirty Readings, in 1866, began and ended at St. James's Hall, Piccadilly. The opening night was that of Tuesday, the 10th of April, the closing night that of Tuesday, the 12th of June. Between those dates half-a-dozen other Readings were given from the same central platform in London, the indefatigable author making his appearance meanwhile alternately in the principal cities of the United Kingdom. Besides revisiting in this way (some of these places repeatedly) in the north, Edinburgh and Glasgow and Aberdeen, in the south and south-west, Clifton and Portsmouth, as well as Liverpool and Manchester intermediately—Charles Dickens during the course of this tour read for the first time at Bristol, at Greenwich, and in the Crystal Palace at Sydenham.

The inauguration of the series of Readings now referred to had a peculiar interest imparted to it by the circumstance that, on the evening of Tuesday, the 10th of April, 1866, there was first of all introduced to public notice the comic patter and pathetic recollections of the Cheap Jack, Doctor Marigold.

Half a year afterwards a longer series of the Readings began under the organisation of the Messrs. Chappell, and under the direction of Mr. Dolby as their business manager. It took place altogether under precisely similar circumstances as the last, with this only difference that the handsome terms of remuneration originally guaranteed to the author were, as already intimated, considerably and voluntarily increased by the projectors of the enterprise, the pecuniary results of the first series having been so very largely beyond their expectations. Fifty Readings instead of thirty were now arranged for—Ireland being visited as well as the principal towns and cities of England and Scotland. Six Readings were given at Dublin, and one at Belfast; four were given at Glasgow, and two at Edinburgh. Bath, for the first time, had the opportunity of according a public welcome to the great humorist, some of the drollest scenes in whose earliest masterpiece occur in the city of Bladud, as every true Pickwickian very well remembers. Then, also, for the first time, he was welcomed—by old admirers of his in his capacity as an author, new admirers of his thenceforth in his later and minor capacity as a Reader—at Swansea and Gloucester, at Stoke and Blackburn, at Hanley and Warrington. Tuesday, the 15th of January, 1867, was the inaugural night of the series, when "Barbox, Brothers," and "The Boy at Mugby," were read for the first time at St. James's Hall, Piccadilly. Monday, the 13th of May, was the date of the last night of the season, which was brought to a close upon the same platform, the success of every Reading, without exception, both in London and in the provinces, having been simply unexampled.

It was shortly after this that the notion was first entertained by the Novelist of entering upon that Reading Tour in America, which has since become so widely celebrated. Overtures had been made to him repeatedly from the opposite shores of the Atlantic, with a view to induce him to give a course of Readings in the United States. Speculators would gladly, no doubt, have availed themselves of so golden an opportunity for turning to account his immense reputation. There were those, however, at home here, who doubted as to the advisability of the author entering, under any conceivable circumstances, upon an undertaking obviously involving in its successful accomplishment an enormous amount of physical labour and excitement. Added to this, the project was inseparable in any case—however favourable might be the manner of its ultimate arrangement—from a profound sense of responsibility all through the period that would have to be set apart for its realisation. It was among the more remarkable characteristics of Charles Dickens that, while he was endowed with a brilliant imagination, and with a genius in many ways incomparable, he was at the same time gifted with the clearest and soundest judgment, being, in point of fact, what is called a thoroughly good man of business. Often as he had shewn this to be the case during the previous phases of his career, he never demonstrated the truth of it so undeniably as in the instance of this proposed Reading Tour in the United States. Determined to understand at once whether the scheme, commended by some, denounced by others, was in itself, to begin with, feasable, and after that advisable, he despatched Mr. Dolby to America for the purpose of surveying the proposed scene of operations. Immediately on his emissary's return, Dickens drew up a few pithy sentences, headed by him, "The Case in a Nutshell." His decision was what those more immediately about him had for some time anticipated. He made up his mind to go, and to go quite independently. The Messrs. Chappell, it should be remarked at once, had no part whatever in the enterprise. The Author-Reader accepted for himself the sole responsibility of the undertaking. As a matter of course, he retained Mr. Dolby as his business manager, despatching him again across the Atlantic, when everything had been arranged between them, to the end that all should be in readiness by the time of his own arrival.

Within the brief interval which then elapsed, between the business manager's return to, and the Author-Reader's departure for, America, that well-remembered Farewell Banquet was given to Charles Dickens, which was not unworthy of signalising his popularity and his reputation. He himself, upon the occasion, spoke of it as that "proud night," recognising clearly enough, as he could hardly fail to do, in the gathering around him, there in Freemasons' Hall, on the evening of the 2nd of November, 1867, one of the most striking incidents in a career that had been almost all sunshine, both from within and from without, from the date of its commencement. It was there, in the midst of what he himself referred to, at the time, as that "brilliant representative company," while acknowledging the presence around him of so many of his brother artists, "not only in literature, but also in the fine arts," he availed himself of the opportunity to relate very briefly the story of his setting out once more for America. "Since I was there before," he said, "a vast, entirely new generation has arisen in the United States. Since I was there before, most of the best known of my books have been written and published. The new generation and the books have come together and have kept together, until at last numbers of those who have so widely and constantly read me, naturally desiring a little variety in the relations between us, have expressed a strong wish that I should read myself. This wish at last conveyed to me, through public channels and business channels, has gradually become enforced by an immense accumulation of letters from individuals and associations of individuals, all expressing in the same hearty, homely, cordial, unaffected way a kind of personal interest in me; I had almost said a kind of personal affection for me, which I am sure you will agree with me, it would be dull insensibility on my part not to prize." Hence, as he explained, his setting forth on that day week upon his second visit to America, with a view among other purposes, according to his own happy phrase, to use his best endeavours "to lay down a third cable of intercommunication and alliance between the old world and the new." The illustrious chairman who presided over that Farewell Banquet, Lord Lytton, had previously remarked, speaking in his capacity as a politician, "I should say that no time could be more happily chosen for his visit;" adding, "because our American kinsfolk have conceived, rightly or wrongfully, that they have some cause of complaint against ourselves, and out of all England we could not have selected an envoy more calculated to allay irritation and to propitiate good will." As one whose cordial genius was, in truth, a bond of sympathy between the two great kindred nationalities, Charles Dickens indeed went forth in one sense at that time, it might almost have been said, in a semi-ambassadorial character, not between the rulers, but between the peoples. The incident of his visit to America could in no respect be considered a private event, but, from first to last, was regarded, and reasonably regarded, as a public and almost as an international occurrence. "Happy is the man," said Lord Lytton, on that 2nd of November, when proposing the toast of the evening in words of eloquence worthy of himself and of his theme, "Happy is the man who makes clear his title deeds to the royalty of genius, while he yet lives to enjoy the gratitude and reverence of those whom he has subjected to his sway. Though it is by conquest that he achieves his throne, he at least is a conqueror whom the conquered bless, and the more despotically he enthralls the dearer he becomes to the hearts of men." Observing, in conclusion, as to this portion of his argument, "Seldom, I say, has that kind of royalty been quietly conceded to any man of genius until his tomb becomes his throne, and yet there is not one of us now present who thinks it strange that it is granted without a murmur to the guest whom we receive to-night." As if in practical recognition of the prerogative thus gracefully referred to by his brother-author, a royal saloon carriage on Friday, the 8th of November, conveyed Charles Dickens from London to Liverpool. On the following morning he took his departure on board the *Cuba* for the United States, arriving at Boston on Tuesday, the 19th, when the laconic message " Safe and well," was flashed home by submarine telegraph.

The Readings projected in America were intended to number up as many as eighty altogether. They actually numbered up exactly Seventy-Six. They were inaugurated by the first of the Boston Readings on Monday, the 2nd of December, 1867. Extending over an interval of less than five months, they closed in Steinway Hall on Monday, the 20th April, 1868, with the last of the New York Readings. From beginning to end, the enthusiasm awakened by these Readings was entirely unparalleled. Simply to ensure a chance of purchasing the tickets of admission, a queue of applicants a quarter of a mile long would pass a whole winter's night patiently waiting in sleet and snow, out in the streets, to be in readiness for the opening of the office-doors when the sale of tickets should have commenced. Blankets and in several instances mattresses were brought with them by some of the more provident of these nocturnal wayfarers, many of whom of course were notoriously middle-men who simply speculated, with immense profit to themselves, in selling again at enormously advanced prices the tickets which were invariably dispensed by the business manager at the fixed charges originally announced.

As curiously illustrative of the first outburst of this enthusiasm even before the Novelist's arrival—on the very eve of that arrival, as it happened—mention may here be made of the simple facts in regard to the sale of tickets on Monday, the 18th of November. During the whole of that day, from the first thing in the morning to the last thing at night, Mr. Dolby sat there at his desk in the Messrs. Ticknor and Fields' book-store, literally doing nothing but sell tickets as fast as he could distribute them and take the money. For thirteen hours together, without taking bite or sup, without ever once for a passing moment quitting the office-stool on which he was perched—fortunately for him behind a strong barricade—he answered the rush of applicants that steadily pressed one another onwards to the pigeon-hole, each drifting by exhausted when his claims were satisfied. The indefatigable manager took in moneys paid down within those thirteen consecutive hours as many as twelve thousand dollars.

During the five months of his stay in America, four Readings a week were given by the Novelist to audiences as numerous as the largest building in each town of a suitable character could by any contrivance be made to contain. The average number of those present upon each of these occasions may be reasonably estimated as at the very least 1500 individuals. Remembering that there were altogether seventy-six Readings, this would show at once that upwards of one hundred thousand souls (114,000) listened to the voice of the great Author reading, what they had so often before read themselves, and raising their own voices in return to greet his ears with their ringing acclamations. At a moderate estimate, again, just as we have seen that each Reading represented 1500 as the average number of the audience, that audience represented, in its turn, in cash, at the lowest computation, nett proceeds amounting to fully $3000. At Rochester, for example, in the State of New York, was the smallest house anywhere met with in the whole course of these American Readings, and even that yielded $2500, the largest house in the tour, on the other hand, netting as much as $6000 and upwards. Multiplying, therefore, the reasonably-mentioned average of $3000 by seventy-six, as the aggregate number of the Readings, we arrive at the astounding result that in this tour of less than five months the Author-Reader netted altogether the enormous sum of $228,000. Supposing gold to have been then at par, that lump sum would have represented in our English currency what if spoken of even in a whisper would, according to Hood's famous witticism, have represented something like "the roar of a Forty Thousand Pounder!" Even as it was, then, gold being at 39½ per cent. premium, with ¼ per cent. more deducted on commission—virtually a drop of nearly 40 per cent. altogether!—the result was the winning of a fortune in what, but for the fatigue involved in it, might have been regarded as simply a holiday excursion.

The fatigue here referred to, however, must have been something very considerable. Its influence was felt all the more, no doubt, by reason of the Novelist having had to contend during upwards of four hard winter months, as he himself laughingly remarked just before his return homewards, with "what he had sometimes been quite admiringly assured, was a true American catarrh!" Nevertheless, even with its depressing and exhausting influence upon him, he not only contrived to carry out the project upon which he had adventured, triumphantly to its appointed close, but even upon one of the most inclement days of an unusually inclement season, namely, on Saturday, the 29th of February, 1868, he actually took part as one of the umpires in the good-humoured frolic of a twelve-mile walking match, up hill and down dale, through the snow, on the Milldam road, between Boston and Newton, doing every inch of the way, heel and toe, as though he had been himself one of the competitors. The first six miles having been accomplished by the successful competitor in one hour and twenty-three minutes, and the return six in one hour and twenty-five minutes, the Novelist—although, with his light, springy step, he had observantly gone the whole distance himself, as we have seen, in his capacity as umpire,—presided blithely, in celebration of this winter day's frolic, at a sumptuous little banquet, given by him at the Parker House, a banquet that Lucullus would hardly have disdained. Having appeared before his last audience in America on the 20th of April, 1868, at New York, the Author-Reader addressed through them to all his other auditors in the United States, after that final Reading was over, a few genial and generous utterances of farewell. Among other things, he said to them,—"The relations which have been set up between us, while they have involved for me something more than mere devotion to a task, have been sustained by you with the readiest sympathy and the kindest acknowledgment. Those relations must now be broken for ever. Be assured, however, that you will not pass from my mind. I shall often realise you as I see you now, equally by my winter fire, and in the green English summer weather. I shall never recall you as a mere audience, but rather as a host of personal friends,—and ever with the greatest gratitude, tenderness, and consideration." Two days before that last of all these American Readings, he had been entertained at a public banquet in New York, on the 18th of April, at Delmonico's. Two days after the final American Reading and address of farewell, he took his departure from New York on board the *Russia*, on Wednesday, the 22nd of April, arriving on Friday, the 1st of May, at Liverpool.

Scarcely a month had elapsed after his return homewards, when the prospective and definitive close of the great author's career as a public Reader was formally announced. Again the Messrs. Chappell, of New Bond Street, appeared between the Novelist and the public as intermediaries. They intimated through their advertisement, that "knowing it to be the determination of Mr. Dickens finally to retire from public Readings, soon after his return from America, they (as having been honoured with his confidence on former occasions) made proposals to him, while he was still in the United States achieving his recent brilliant successes there, for a final farewell series of Readings in this country." They added that "their proposals were at once accepted in a manner highly gratifying to them;" and that the series, which would commence in the ensuing autumn, would comprehend, besides London, several of the chief towns and cities of England, Ireland, and Scotland. Looking back to this preliminary advertisement now, there is a melancholy significance in the emphasis with which it was observed—"It is scarcely necessary to add that any announcement made in connection with these Farewell Readings will be strictly adhered to and considered final; and that on no consideration whatever will Mr. Dickens be induced to appoint an extra night in any place in which he shall have been announced to read for the last time." According to promise, in the autumn, these well-remembered Farewell Readings commenced. They were intended to run on to the number of one hundred altogether. Beginning within the first week of October, they were not to end until the third week of the ensuing May. As it happened, Seventy-Four Readings were given in place of the full hundred. On Tuesday, the 6th of October, 1868, the series was commenced. On Thursday, the 22nd of April, 1869, its abrupt termination was announced, by a telegram from Preston, that caused a pang of grief and anxiety to the vast multitude of those to whom the very name of Charles Dickens had, for more than thirty years, been endeared. The intimation conveyed through that telegram was the fact of his sudden and alarming illness. Already, in the two preceding months, though the public generally had taken no notice of the circumstance, three of the Readings had, for various reasons, been unavoidably given up—one at Hull, fixed for the 12th of March, and previously one at Glasgow, fixed for the 18th, and another at Edinburgh, fixed for the 19th of February. Otherwise than in those three instances, the sequence of Readings marked on the elaborate programme had been most faithfully adhered to; the Reader, indeed, only succumbing at last under the nervous exhaustion caused by his own indomitable perseverance.

It is, now, matter of all but absolute certainty that his immense energies, his elastic temperament, and his splendid constitution had all of them, long before this, been cruelly overtaxed and overweighted. Unsuspected by any of us at the time, he had, there can be little doubt of it, received the deadliest shock to his whole system as far back as on the 9th of June, 1865, in that terrible railway accident at Staplehurst, on the fifth anniversary of which fatal day, by a strange coincidence, he breathed his last. His intense vitality deceived himself and everybody else, however, until it was all too late. The extravagant toil he was going through for months together—whirling hither and thither in express trains, for the purpose of making one exciting public appearance after another, each of them a little world of animated impersonations—he accomplished with such unfailing and unflagging vivacity, with such an easy step, such an alert carriage, with such an animated voice and glittering eye, that for a long while at least we were under the illusion. Hurrying about England, Ireland, and Scotland as he was during almost the whole of the last quarter of 1868 and during the whole of the first quarter of 1869—dividing his time not only between Liverpool and Manchester, Edinburgh and Glasgow, Dublin and Belfast, with continual returns to his central reading-platform in the great Hall near Piccadilly, but visiting afterwards as well nearly all the great manufacturing towns and nearly all the fashionable watering-places—the wonder is now not so much that he gave in at last to the exorbitant strain, but that he did not give in much sooner.

A single incident will suffice to show the pace at which he was going before the overwrought system gave the first sign of its *being* overwrought. On the evening of Thursday, the 11th of March, 1869, an immense audience crowded the Festival Concert Room at York, the people there having only that one opportunity of attending a Farewell Reading. As they entered the room, each person received a printed slip of paper, on which was read, "The audience are respectfully informed that carriages have been ordered to-night at half-past nine. Without altering his Reading in the least, Mr. Dickens will shorten his usual pauses between the Parts, in order that he may leave York by train a few minutes after that time. He has been summoned," it was added, "to London, in connection with a late sad occurrence within the general knowledge, but a more particular reference to which would be out of place here." His attendance, in point of fact, was suddenly required at the funeral of a dear friend of his in the metropolis. To the funeral he had to go. From the poignantly irksome duty of the Reading he could not escape. Giving the latter even as proposed, he would barely have time to catch the up express, so as to arrive in town by the aid of rapid night travelling, and be true to the melancholy rendezvous at the scene of his friend's obsequies. The Readings that night were three, and they were given in rapid succession, the Reader, after the first and second, instead of withdrawing, as usual, for ten minutes' rest into his retiring room at the back of the platform, merely stepping for an instant or two behind the screen at the side of the platform, putting his lips to some iced champagne, and stepping back at once to the reading-desk. The selected Readings were these—"Boots at the Holly-Tree Inn," the murder scene of "Sikes and Nancy," and the grotesque monologue of "Mrs. Gamp." The Archbishop and the other principal people of York were there conspicuously noticeable in the stalls, eagerly listening and keenly observant, evidently in rapt attention throughout the evening, but more especially during the powerfully acted tragic incident from "Oliver Twist." The Reading, as a whole, was more than ordinarily successful—parts of it were exceptionally impressive. Directly it was over, the Reader, having had a *coupé* previously secured for his accommodation in the express, was just barely enabled, at a rush, to catch the train an instant or so before its starting. Then only, after it had started, could he give a thought to his dress, changing his clothes and snatching a morsel of supper in the railway carriage as he whirled on towards London. The occasion referred to serves, at any rate, to illustrate the wear and tear to which the Author had rendered himself, through these Readings, more or less continually liable.

The jeopardy in which it placed his life at last was alarmingly indicated by the peremptory order of his medical adviser, Mr. Frank Beard, of Welbeck Street—immediately on his arrival in Preston on the 22nd of April, in answer to a telegram summoning him thither upon the instant from London—that the Readings must be stopped then and thenceforth. When this happened, a fortnight had not elapsed after the grand Banquet given in honour of Charles Dickens at St. George's Hall, in Liverpool. As the guest of the evening, he had, there and then, been "cheered to the echo" by seven hundred enthusiastic admirers of his, presided over by the Mayor of Liverpool. That was on Saturday, the 10th of April, during a fortnight's blissful rest in the whirling round of the Readings. Immediately that fortnight was over, the whirling round began again its momentarily interrupted gyrations. Three days in succession there was a Reading at Leeds—on Thursday, the 15th, Friday, the 16th, and Saturday, the 17th of April. On Monday, the 19th, there was a Reading at Blackburn; on Tuesday, the 20th, another at Bolton; on Wednesday, the 21st, another at Southport. Then came the morning of the 22nd, on the evening of which Thursday he was to have read at Preston. By the time Dickens's medical adviser had arrived from London, the audience had already begun assembling. Thereupon, not only was that particular Reading prohibited, but, by the same wise mandate, all thought of resuming the course, or even a portion of it, afterwards, was as peremptorily interdicted. In one sense, it is only matter for wistful regret, now, that that judicious interdict was so far removed, three-quarters of a year afterwards, that the twelve Final Readings of Farewell which were given at the St. James' Hall in the spring of 1870, beginning on Tuesday, the 11th of January, and ending on Tuesday, the 15th of March, were assented to as in any way reasonable.

That even these involved an enormous strain upon the system, was proved to absolute demonstration by the statistics jotted down with the utmost precision during the Readings, as to the fluctuations of the Reader's pulse immediately before and immediately after each of his appearances upon the platform, mostly two, but often three, appearances in a single evening. The acceleration of his pulse has, to our knowledge, upon some of these occasions been something extraordinary. Upon the occasion of his last and grandest Reading of the Murder, for example, as he stepped upon the platform, resolved, apparently, upon outdoing himself, he remarked, in a half-whisper to the present writer, just before advancing from the cover of the screen to the familiar reading-desk, "I shall tear myself to pieces." He certainly never acted with more impassioned earnestness—though never once, for a single instant, however, overstepping the boundaries of nature. His pulse just before had been tested, as usual, keenly and carefully, by his most sedulous and sympathetic medical attendant. It was counted by him just as keenly and carefully directly afterwards—the rise then apparent being something startling, almost alarming, as it seemed to us under the circumstances.

Those twelve Farewell Readings are all the more to

be regretted now when we come to look back at them, on our recalling to remembrance the fact that then, for the first time since he assumed to himself the position of a Public Reader professionally, Dickens consented to give a series of Readings at the very period when he was producing one of his imaginative works in monthly instalments. He appeared to give himself no rest whatever, when repose, at any rate for a while, was most urgently required. He seemed to have become his own taskmaster precisely at the time when he ought to have taken the repose he had long previously earned, by ministering so largely and laboriously to the world's enjoyment.

Summing up in a few words what has already been related in detail, one passing sentence may here recall to recollection the fact, that in addition to the various works produced by the Novelist during the last three lustres of his energetic life as a man of letters, he had personally, within that busy interval of fifteen years, given in round numbers at a moderate computation some 500 of these Public Readings—423 in a strictly professional capacity, the rest, prior to 1858, purely out of motives of generosity, in his character as a practical philanthropist. In doing this he had addressed as many as five hundred enormous audiences, whose rapt attention he had always secured, and who had one and all of them, without exception, welcomed his coming and going with enthusiasm. During this period he had travelled over many thousands of miles, by railway and steam-packet. In a single tour, that of the winter of 1867 and 1868, in America, he had appeared before upwards of 100,000 persons, earning, at the same time, over 200,000 dollars within an interval of very little more than four months altogether.

Later on, the circumstances surrounding the immediate close of this portion of the popular author's life, as a Public Reader of his own works, will be described when mention is made of his final appearance in St. James's Hall, on the night of his Farewell Reading. Before any particular reference is made, however, to that last evening, it may be advisable, as tending to make this record more complete, that there should now be briefly passed in review, one after another, those minor stories, and fragments of the larger stories, the simple recounting of which by his own lips yielded so much artistic delight to a great multitude of his contemporaries. Whatever may thus be remarked in regard to these Readings will be written at least from a vivid personal recollection; the writer, throughout, speaking, as before observed, from his intimate knowledge of the whole of this protracted episode in the life of the Novelist.

Whatever aid to the memory besides might have been thought desirable, he has had ready to hand all through, in the marked copies of the very books from which the author read upon these occasions, or from which, at the least, he had the appearance of reading. For, especially towards the last, Charles Dickens hardly ever glanced, even momentarily, at the printed pages, simply turning the leaves mechanically as they lay open before him on the picturesque little reading-desk. Besides the Sixteen Readings actually given, there were Four others which were so far meditated that they were printed separately as "Readings," though the reading copies of them that have been preserved, were never otherwise prepared by their author-compiler for representation. One of these the writer remembers suggesting to the Novelist, as a characteristic companion or contrast to Dr. Marigold,—meaning "Mrs. Lirriper." Another, strange to say,—about the least likely of all his stories one would have thought to have been thus selected,—was "The Haunted Man." A third was "The Prisoner of the Bastile," which would, for certain, have been one of Dickens's most powerful delineations. The fourth, if only in remembrance of the Old Bailey attorney, Mr. Jaggers, of the convict Magwitch, and of Joe the blacksmith, the majority would probably have been disposed to regret almost more than Mrs. Lirriper. Though the lodging-house keeper would have been welcome, too, for her own sake, as who will not agree in saying, if merely out of a remembrance of the "trembling lip" put up towards her face, speaking of which the good motherly old soul exclaims, "and I dearly kissed it;" or, bearing in mind, another while, her preposterous reminiscence of the "impertinent little cock-sparrow of a monkey whistling with dirty shoes on the clean steps, and playing the harp on the area railings with a hoop-stick." Actually given or only meditated, the whole of these twenty Readings—meaning the entire collection of the identical marked copies used by the Novelist himself on both sides of the Atlantic—have, for the verification of this retrospect, been placed for the time being in the writer's possession. Selecting from among them those merely which are familiar to the public, from their having been actually produced, he here proposes cursorily to glance one by one through the well-known series of Sixteen.

THE CHRISTMAS CAROL.

It can hardly be any matter for wonder that the "Christmas Carol" was, among all the Readings, the author's own especial favourite! That it was so, he showed from first to last unmistakeably. He began with it in 1853, and ended with it in 1870, upon the latter occasion appending to the long since abbreviated narrative, that other incomparable evidence of his powers as a humorist, "The Trial from Pickwick." Whoever went for the first time to see and hear Charles Dickens read one or other of his writings, did well in selecting a night when he was going to relate his immortal ghost story of Christmas. In compliance with the well-known wish of the Novelist, the audience, as a rule, contrived to assemble and to have actually taken their places several minutes before the time fixed for the Reader's appearance upon the platform. Occasionally it happened, nevertheless, that a stray couple or so would be still drifting in, here and there, among the serried ranks of the stalls, when, book in hand, with a light step, a smile on his face, and a flower in his button-hole, the author had already rapidly advanced and taken his place before his quaintly constructed but graceful little reading-desk. Then it was, perhaps, at those very times, that a stranger to the whole scene regarded himself almost as under a personal obligation to these vexatious stragglers. For, until every one of them had quietly settled down, there stood the Novelist, cheerfully, patiently, glancing to the right and to the left, taking the bearings of his night's company, as one might say, with an air of the most perfect ease and self-possession. Whosoever, consequently, was in attendance there for the first time, had an opportunity, during any such momentary pause, of familiarising himself with the appearance of the famous writer, with whose books he had probably been intimately acquainted for years upon years previously, but whom until then he had never had the chance of beholding face to face.

Everyone, even to the illiterate wayfarers in the public streets, had, to a certain extent, long since come to know what manner of man Charles Dickens was by means of his widely-scattered photographs. But, there, better than any photograph, was the man himself,—the master of all English humorists, the most popular author during his own lifetime that ever existed; one whose stories for thirty years together had been read with tears and with laughter, and whose books had won for him personal affection, as well as fame and fortune. Anyone seeing him at those moments for the first time, would unquestionably think—How like he was to a very few indeed, how utterly unlike the vast majority of his countless cartes-de-visites! To the last there was the bright, animated, alert carriage of the head—phrenologically a noble head—physiognomically a noble countenance. Encountering him within a very few weeks of his death, Mr. Arthur Locker has said, "I was especially struck with the brilliancy and vivacity of his eyes:" adding, "there seemed as much life and animation in them as in twenty ordinary pairs of eyes." Another keen observer, Mr. Arthur Helps, has in the same spirit exclaimed, "What portrait can do justice to the frankness, kindness, and power of his eyes?" None certainly that ever was painted by the pencil of the sunbeam, or by the brush of a Royal Academician. Fully to realise the capacity for indicating emotion latent in them, and informing his whole frame—his hands for example, in their every movement, being wonderfully expressive—those who attended these Readings soon came to know, that you had but to listen to his variable and profoundly sympathetic voice, and to watch the play of his handsome features.

The different original characters introduced in his stories, when he read them, he did not simply describe, he impersonated: otherwise to put it, for whomsoever he spoke, he spoke in character. Thus, when everything was quiet in the crowded assembly, and when the ringing applause that always welcomed his appearance, but which he never by any chance acknowledged, had subsided—when he began: "A Christmas Carol, in four staves. Stave one, Marley's Ghost. Marley was dead to begin with." Having remarked, yet further, that "there was no doubt whatever about that," the register of his burial being signed by this functionary, that and the other—when he added, "*Scrooge* signed it; and Scrooge's name was good upon 'Change for anything he chose to put his hand to"—Scrooge in the flesh was, through the very manner of the utterance of his name, brought vividly and upon the instant before the observant listener. "Oh! but he was a tight-fisted hand at the grindstone, was Scrooge!" *That* we knew instinctively, without there being any need whatever for our hearing one syllable of the description of him, admirably given in the book, but suppressed in the Reading, judiciously suppressed enough, because, for that matter, we saw and heard it without any necessity for its being explained. As one might say—quoting here a single morsel from the animated description of Scrooge, that was actually illustrated by Scrooge's impersonator—it all "spoke out shrewdly in his grating voice!" And it was thus, not merely with regard to the leading personages of the little acted drama, as, turn by turn, they were introduced; precisely the same artistic care was applied by the impersonating realist to the very least among the minor characters, filling in, so to speak, little incidental gaps in the background. A great fat man with a monstrous chin, for example, was introduced just momentarily in the briefest street-dialogue, towards the close of this very Reading, who had only to open his lips once or twice for an instant, yet whose individuality was in that instant or two so thoroughly realised, that he lives ever since then in the hearers' remembrance. When, in reply to some one's inquiry, as to what was the cause of Scrooge's (presumed) death?—this great fat man with the monstrous chin answered, with a yawn, in two words, "God knows!" —he was before us there, as real as life, as selfish, and as substantial. So was it also with the grey-haired rascal, Joe, of the rag-and-bottle shop; with Topper, when he pronounced himself, as a bachelor, to be "a wretched outcast;" with the Schoolmaster, when he "glared on Master Scrooge with ferocious condescension, and threw him into a dreadful state of mind by shaking hands with him," all of whom were indicated by the merest touch or two, and yet each of whom was a living and breathing and speaking verisimilitude.

There was produced, to begin with, however, a sense of exhilaration in the very manner with which Dickens commenced the Reading of one of his stories, and which was always especially noticeable in the instance of this particular ghost story of his about Christmas. The opening sentences were always given in those cheery, comfortable tones, indicative of a double relish on the part of a narrator—to wit, his own enjoyment of the tale he is going to relate, and his anticipation of the enjoyment of it by those who are giving him their attention. Occasionally, at any rate during the last few years, his voice was husky just at the commencement, but as he warmed to his work, with him at all times a genuine labour of love, everything of that kind disappeared almost at the first turn of the leaf. The genial inflections of the voice, curiously rising, in those first moments of the Reading, at the end of every sentence, there was simply no resisting. Had there been a wedding guest present, he would hardly have repined in not being able to obey the summons of the loud bassoon. The narrator had his will with one and all. However large and however miscellaneous the audience, from the front of the stalls to the back of the gallery, every one listened to the familiar words that fell from his lips, from the beginning to the end, with unflagging attention. There could be small room for marvel at this, however, in the instance of the "Carol," on first reading which, Thackeray spoke of its author as that "delightful genius!" The *Edinburgh* editor, Lord Jeffrey, at the very same time, namely, towards the close of 1843, on the morrow of the little book's original publication, avowing, in no less glowing terms, that he had been nothing less than charmed by the exquisite apologue: "chiefly," as he declared, "for the genuine goodness which breathes all through it, and is the true inspiring angel by which its genius has been awakened." Never since he had first—and that but a very few years previously—taken pen in hand as a story-teller, had this "delightful genius" sat down in a happier vein for writing anything, than when he did so for the purpose of recounting how Scrooge was converted, by a series of ghostly apparitions, from the error of his utterly selfish way in life, until then, as a tough-skinned, ingrained curmudgeon.

Characters and incidents, brought before us anew in the Reading, were all so cordially welcomed,—the former being such old friends, the latter so familiarly within our knowledge! Insomuch that many passages were, almost word for word, remembered by those who, nevertheless, listened as if curious to learn what might follow, yet who could readily, any one of them, have prompted the Reader, that is the Author himself, supposing by some rare chance he had happened, just for one moment, to be at fault. It is curious to observe, on turning over the leaves of the marked copy of this Reading, the sententious little marginal notes for his own guidance, jotted down by the hand of this wonderful master of elocutionary effect. "Narrative" is written on the side of p. 5 where Scrooge's office, on Christmas Eve, is described, just before mention is made of the Clerk's dismal little cell seeming to be "a sort of tank," and of his fire being so small that it looked like "one coal," and of his trying at last to warm himself by the candle, "in which effort, not being a man of strong imagination, he failed." Again, "Cheerful" is penned on the side of p. 6, where Scrooge's Nephew comes in at a burst with "A Merry Christmas, uncle! God save you!"

After Scrooge's inhuman retort of "Bah! humbug!" not a word was added of the descriptive sentence immediately following. Admirable though every word of it is, however, one could hardly regret its suppression. Is it asked why? Well then, for this simple reason — the force of which will be admitted by anyone who ever had the happiness of grasping Charles Dickens's hand in friendship—that his description of Scrooge's Nephew was, quite unconsciously but most accurately, in every word of it, a literal description of himself, just as he looked upon any day in the blithest of all seasons, after a brisk walk in the wintry streets or on the snowy high road. "He had so heated himself with rapid walking in the fog and frost, this Nephew of Scrooge's, that he was all in a glow; his face was ruddy and handsome; his eyes sparkled, and his breath smoked again." The Novelist himself was depicted there to a nicety. No need, therefore, was there for even one syllable of this in the Reading. Scrooge's Nephew was visibly before us, without a word being uttered.

To our thinking, it has always seemed as if the one chink through which Scrooge's sympathies are got at and his heart-strings are eventually touched, is discernable in his keen sense of humour from the very outset. It is precisely through this that there seems hope, from the very beginning, of his proving to be made of "penetrable stuff." When, after his monstrous "Out upon merry Christmas!" he goes on to say, "If I had my will every idiot who goes about with 'merry Christmas' on his lips should be boiled with his own pudding and buried with a stake of holly in his heart: he should!" one almost feels as if he were laughing in his sleeve from the very commencement. Instance, as yet more strikingly to the point in respect to what we are here maintaining, the wonderfully comic effect of the bantering remarks addressed by him to the Ghost of Jacob Marley all through their confabulation, even when the spectre's voice, as we are told, was disturbing the very marrow in his bones. True, it is there stated that, all through that portentous dialogue, he was only trying to be smart "as a means of distracting his own attention." But the jests themselves are too delicious, one would say, for mere make-believes. Besides which, hear his laugh at the end of the book! Hardly that of one really so long out of practice—"a splendid laugh, a most illustrious laugh, the father of a long, long line of brilliant laughs!" A laugh, one might suppose, as contagious as that of his own Nephew when he was "so inexpressibly tickled that he was obliged to get up off the sofa and stamp!" Speaking of which our author writes so delectably, "If you should happen by any unlikely chance to know a man more blest in a laugh than Scrooge's Nephew, all I can say is, I should like to know him too. Introduce him to me, and I'll cultivate his acquaintance." At which challenge one might almost have been tempted anticipatively to say at a venture—Scrooge! Good-humoured argument apart, however, what creatures were those who, one by one—sometimes, it almost seemed, two or three of them together—appeared and disappeared upon the platform, at the Reader's own good-will and pleasure!

After Scrooge's "Good afternoon!"—delivered with irresistibly ludicrous iteration—we caught something more than a distant glimpse of the Clerk in the tank, when—on Scrooge's surly interrogation, if he will want all day to-morrow?—the Reader replied in the thinnest and meekest of frightened voices, "If quite convenient, sir!" It brought into full view instantaneously, and for the first time, the little Clerk whom one followed in imagination with interest a minute afterwards on his "going down a slide at the end of a lane of boys twenty times in honour of Christmas, and then, with the long ends of his white comforter dangling below his waist (for he boasted no greatcoat) running home as hard as he could pelt to play at blind man's buff." Instantly, upon the heels of this, we find noted on the margin, p. 18, "Tone to mystery." The spectral illusion of the knocker on Scrooge's house-door, looking for all the world not like a knocker, but like Marley's face, "with a dismal light about it like a bad lobster in a dark cellar," prepared the way marvellously for what followed. Numberless little tid-bits of description that anybody else would have struck out with reluctance, as, for instance, that of Scrooge looking cautiously behind the street door when he entered, "as if he half expected to be terrified with the sight of Marley's pigtail sticking out into the hall," were unhesitatingly erased by the Reader, as, from his point of view, not necessarily to the purpose. Then, after the goblin incident of the disused bell slowly oscillating until it and all the other bells in the house rang loudly for a while—afterwards becoming in turn just as suddenly hushed—we got to the clanking approach, from the sub-basement of the old building, of the noise that at length came on through the heavy door of Scrooge's apartment! "And"—as the Reader said with startling effect, while his voice rose to a hurried outcry as he uttered the closing exclamation—"upon its coming in, the dying flame leaped up, as though it cried, '*I know him! Marley's Ghost!*'" The apparition, although the description of it was nearly stenographically abbreviated in the Reading, appeared to be, in a very few words, no less startlingly realised. "Same face, usual waistcoat, tights, boots," even to the spectral illusion being so transparent that Scrooge (his own marrow, then, we may presume, becoming sensitized) looking through his waistcoat "could see the two back buttons on the coat behind"—with the incorrigible old joker's cynical reflection to himself that "he had often heard Marley spoken of as having no bowels, but had never believed it until then." The grotesque humour of his interview with the spectre seemed scarcely to have been realised, in fact, until their colloquy was actually listened to in the Reading.

Scrooge's entreaty addressed to the Ghost, when the latter demanded a hearing, "Don't be flowery, Jacob, pray!" was only less laughable, for example, than the expression of the old dreamer's visage when Marley informed him that he had often sat beside him invisibly! Promised a chance and hope in the future —a chance and hope of his dead partner's procuring— Scrooge's "Thank 'ee!"—full of doubt—was a fitting prelude to his acknowledgment of the favour when explained. "You will be haunted," quoth the Ghost, "by three Spirits." The other faltering, "I—I think I'd rather not:" and then quietly hinting afterwards, "Couldn't I take 'em all at once, and have it over, Jacob?"

As for the revelations made to Ebenezer Scrooge by those three memorable Spirits of Christmas Past, Present, and Future, who can ever hope to relate them and impersonate them as they were related and impersonated by the Author himself of this peerless ghost-story! Fezziwig, for example, with his calves shining like moons, who, after going through all the intricacies of the country dance, bow, corkscrew, thread-the-needle, and back again to your place, cut—"cut so deftly that he appeared to wink with his legs, and came upon his feet again without a stagger!" The very Fiddler, who "went up to the lofty desk and made an orchestra of it, and tuned like fifty stomach-aches!" Master Peter Cratchit, again, arrayed in his father's shirt collars, who, rejoicing to find himself so gallantly attired, at one moment "yearned to show his linen in the fashionable parks," and at another, hearing his sister Martha talk of some lord who "was much about as tall as Peter, pulled up his collars so high that you couldn't have seen him if you had been there." As for the pathetic portions of the narrative, it is especially observable in regard to those, that they were anything rather than made too much of. There, more particularly, the elisions were ruthless. Looking through the marked copy, it really would appear that only a very few indeed of the salient points were left in regard to the life and death of Tiny Tim. Bob's visit to the death-bed was entirely unmentioned. Even the words "Spirit of Tiny Tim, thy childish essence was from God!" were never uttered. Two utterances there *were*, however, the one breathing an exquisite tenderness, the other indicative of a long-suppressed but passionate outburst of grief, that thrilled to the hearts of all who heard them, and still, we doubt not, haunt their recollection. The one—where the mother, laying her mourning needlework upon the table, put her hand up to her face. "'The colour hurts my eyes,' she said. The colour? *Ah!* poor Tiny Tim!" The other, where the father, while describing the little creature's grave, breaks down in a sudden agony of tears. "It would have done you good to see how green a place it is. But you'll see it often. I promised him that I would walk there on a Sunday—*My little, little child! My little child!*" It was a touch of nature that made the Reader and his world of hearers, upon the instant, kin. The tearful outcry brimmed to the eyes of those present a thousand visible echoes. "He broke down all at once. He couldn't help it," said the Reader, adding in subdued accents the simple words, "If he could have helped it, he and his child would have been further apart perhaps than they were." With that ended all reference to the home-grief at Bob Cratchit's. Everything else in relation to the loss of Tiny Tim was foregone unhesitatingly.

The descriptive passages were cut out by wholesale. While the Christmas dinner at Scrooge's Clerk's, and the Christmas party at Scrooge's Nephew's, were left in almost in their entirety, the street-scenes and shop-window displays were obliterated altogether. Nothing at all was said about the "great round, pot-bellied baskets of chestnuts, shaped like the waistcoats of jolly old gentlemen lolling at the doors and tumbling into the streets in their apoplectic opulence." Nothing about the ruddy, brown-faced, broad-girthed Spanish onions, shining in the fatness of their growth like Spanish friars, and "winking from their shelves in wanton slyness at the girls as they went by, and glanced demurely at the hung-up mistletoe." Nothing about the canisters of tea and coffee "rattled up and down like juggling tricks," or about the candied fruits "so caked and spotted with molten sugar as to make the coldest lookers-on feel faint, and subsequently bilious."

Nay, we were denied even a momentary glimpse, on the snow-crusted pavement at nightfall, of that group of handsome girls, all hooded and fur-booted, and all chattering at once, tripping lightly off to some near neighbour's house, "where, woe upon the single man who saw them enter—artful witches, well they knew it—in a glow!" Topper was there, however, and the plump sister in the lace tucker, and the game of Yes-and-No, the solution to which was, "It's your uncle Scro-o-o-o-oge!" Happiest of all these non-omissions, as one may call them, there was that charming picture of Scrooge's niece by marriage, which—as brightly, exquisitely articulated by the lips of her imaginer—was like the loveliest girl-portrait ever painted by Greuze. "She was very pretty, exceedingly pretty. With a dimpled, surprised-looking, capital face; a ripe little mouth, that seemed made to be kissed—as no doubt it was; all kinds of good little dots about her chin, that melted into one another when she laughed; and the sunniest pair of eyes you ever saw in any little creature's head. Altogether she was what you would have called provoking, you know; but satisfactory, too. Oh, perfectly satisfactory." The grave face and twinkling eyes with which this cordial acquiescence in the conclusion arrived at was expressed were irresistibly exhilarating. Just in the same way there was a sort of parenthetical smack of the lips in the self-communing of Scrooge when, at the very close of the story, after hesitating awhile at his Nephew's door as to whether he should knock, he made a dash and did it. "Is your master at home, my dear?" said Scrooge. "*Nice girl! very.*" Then, as to the cordiality of his reception by his Nephew, what could by possibility have expressed it better than the look, voice, manner of the Reader. "'Will you let me in, Fred?' *Let him in! It is a mercy he didn't shake his arm off.*" The turkey that "never could have stood upon its legs, that bird," but must have "snapped 'em short off in a minute, like sticks of sealing-wax!"—the remarkable boy who was just about its size, and who, when told to go and buy it, cried out "Walk-ER!"—Bob Cratchit's trying to overtake nine o'clock with his pen on his arriving nearly twenty minutes afterwards; his trembling and getting a little nearer the ruler when regenerated Scrooge talks about raising his salary, prior to calling him Bob, and, with a clap on the back, wishing him a merry Christmas!—brought, hilariously, the whole radiant Reading of this wonderful story to its conclusion. It was a feast of humour and a flow of fun, better than all the yule-tide fare that ever was provided—fuller of good things than any Christmas pudding of plums and candied fruit-peel—more warming to the cockles of one's heart, whatever those may be, than the mellowest wassail-bowl ever brimmed to over-flowing. No wonder those two friends of Thackeray, who have been already mentioned, and who were both of them women, said of the Author of the "Carol," by way of criticism, "God bless him!" This being exclaimed by them, as will be remembered, simply after reading it to themselves. If only they had heard him read it!

THE TRIAL FROM PICKWICK.

READER and audience about equally, one may say, revelled in the "Trial from Pickwick." Every well-known person in the comic drama was looked for eagerly, and when at last Serjeant Buzfuz, as we were told, "rose with more importance than he had yet exhibited, if that were possible, and said, 'Call Samuel Weller,'" a round of applause invariably greeted the announcement of perhaps the greatest of all Dickens's purely humorous characters. The Reading copy of this abbreviated report of the great case of *Bardell* v. *Pickwick* has, among the complete set of Readings, one very striking peculiarity. Half-bound in scarlet morocco like all the other thin octavos in the collection, its leaves though yellow and worn with constant turning like the rest, are wholly *un*like those of the others in this, that the text is untouched by pen or pencil. Beyond the first condensation of that memorable 34th chapter of Pickwick, there is introduced not one single alteration by way of after-thought. Struck off at a heat, as it was, that first humorous report of the action for breach of promise of marriage brought by

Martha Bardell against Samuel Pickwick admitted in truth in no way whatever of improvement. Anything like a textual change would have been resented by the hearers—every one of them Pickwickian, as the case might be, to a man, woman, or child—as in the estimation of the literary court, nothing less than a high crime and misdemeanour. Once epitomised for the Reading, the printed version, at least of the report, was left altogether intact. Nevertheless, strange to say, there was perhaps no Reading out of the whole series of sixteen, in the delivery of which the Author more readily indulged himself with an occasional gag. Every interpolation of this kind, however, was so obviously introduced on the spur of the moment, so refreshingly spontaneous and so ludicrously *apropos*, that it was always cheered to the very echo, or, to put the fact not conventionally but literally, was received with peals of laughter. Thus it was in one instance, as we very well remember, in regard to Mr. Justice Stareleigh—upon every occasion that we saw him, one of the Reader's most whimsical impersonations. The little judge—described in the book as "all face and waistcoat"—was presented to view upon the platform as evidently with no neck at all (to speak of), and as blinking with owl-like stolidity whenever he talked, which he always did under his voice, and with apparently a severe cold in the head. On the night more particularly referred to, Sam Weller, being at the moment in the witness-box, had just replied to the counsel's suggestion, that what he (Sam) meant by calling Mr. Pickwick's "a very good service" was "little to do and plenty to get."—"Oh, quite enough to get, sir, as the soldier said ven they ordered him three hundred and fifty lashes." Thereupon—glowering angrily at Sam, and blinking his eyes more than ever—Mr. Justice Stareleigh remarked, with a heavier cold in the head than hitherto, in a severe monotone, and with the greatest deliberation, "You must not tell us what the soldier says unless the soldier is in court, unless that soldier comes here in uniform, and is examined in the usual way—it's not evidence." Another evening, again, we recall quite as clearly to mind, when the Reader was revelling more even than was his wont, in the fun of this representation of the trial-scene, he suddenly seemed to open up the revelation of an entirely new phase in Mr. Winkle's idiosyncrasy. Under the badgering of Mr. Skimpin's irritating examination, as to whether he was or was not a particular friend of Mr. Pickwick the defendant, the usually placable Pickwickian's patience upon this occasion appeared gradually and at last utterly to forsake him. "I have known Mr. Pickwick now, as well as I can recollect at this moment, nearly——" "Pray, Mr. Winkle, do not evade the question. Are you or are you not a particular friend of the defendant's?" "I was just about to say——" "Will you, or will you not, answer my question, sir?" "Why, God bless my soul, I was just about to say that——" Whereupon the Court, otherwise Mr. Justice Stareleigh, blinking faster than ever, blurted out severely, "If you don't answer the question you'll be committed to prison, sir!" And then, but not till then, Mr. Winkle was sufficiently restored to equanimity to admit at last, meekly, "Yes, he was!"

In the Reading of the Trial the first droll touch was the well-remembered reference to the gentlemen in wigs, in the barristers' seats, presenting as a body "all that pleasing variety of nose and whisker for which the bar of England is so justly celebrated." Even the allusion to those among their number who carried a brief "scratching their noses with it to impress the fact more strongly on the observation of the spectators," and the other allusion to those who hadn't a brief, carrying instead red-labelled octavos with "that under-done-pie-crust cover, technically known as law calf," was each, in turn, welcomed with a flutter of amusement. Every point, however minute, told, and told effectively. More effectively than if each was heard for the first time, because all were thoroughly known, and, therefore, thoroughly well appreciated. The opening address of Serjeant Buzfuz every one naturally enough regarded as one of the most mirth-moving portions of the whole representation. In the very exordium of it there was something eminently absurd in the Serjeant's extraordinarily precise, almost mincing pronunciation. As where he said, that "never in the whole course of his professional experience—never from the first moment of his applying himself to the study and practice of the law—had he approached a case with such a heavy sense of respon-see-bee-lee-ty imposed upon him—a respon-see-bee-lee-ty he could never have supported were he not," and so forth. Again, a wonderfully ridiculous effect was imparted by the Reader to his mere contrasts of manner when, at one moment, in the bland and melancholy accents of Serjeant Buzfuz, he referred to the late Mr. Bardell as having "glided almost imperceptibly from the world to seek elsewhere for that repose and peace which a custom-house can never afford," adding, the next instant in his own voice, and with the most cruelly matter-of-fact precision, "This was a pathetic description of the decease of Mr. Bardell, who had been knocked on the head with a quart-pot in a public-house cellar." The gravity of the Reader's countenance at these moments, with, now and then, but very rarely, a lurking twinkle in the eye, was of itself irresistibly provocative of laughter. Even upon the Serjeant's mention of the written placard hung up in the parlour window of Goswell Street, bearing this inscription, "Apartments furnished for single gentlemen: inquire within," the sustained seriousness with which he added, that there the forensic orator paused while several gentlemen of the jury "took a note of the document," one of that intelligent body inquiring, "There is no date to that, is there, sir?" made fresh ripples of laughter spread from it as inevitably as the concentric circles on water from the dropping of a pebble. The crowning extravagances of this most Gargantuan of comic orations were always of course the most eagerly welcomed, such, for example, as the learned Serjeant's final allusion to Pickwick's coming before the court that day with "his heartless tomato-sauce and warming-pans," and the sonorous close of the impassioned peroration with the plaintiff's appeal to "an enlightened, a high-minded, a right-feeling, a conscientious, a dispassionate, a sympathising, a contemplative jury of her civilised countrymen." It was after this, however, that the true fun of the Reading began with the examination and cross-examination of the different witnesses. These, as a matter of course, were acted, not described.

Mrs. Cluppins first entered the box, with her feelings, so far as they could be judged from her voice, evidently all but too many for her. Her fluttered reply showed this at the very commencement, in answer to an inquiry as to whether she remembered one particular morning in July last, when Mrs. Bardell was dusting Pickwick's apartment. "Yes, my lord and jury, I do." "Was that sitting-room the first-floor front?" "Yes, it were, sir"—something in the manner of Mrs. Crupp when at her faintest. The suspicious inquiry of the red-faced little Judge, "What were you doing in the back-room, ma'am?" followed—on her replying lackadaisically, "My lord and jury, I will not deceive you"—by his blinking at her more fiercely, "You had better not, ma'am," were only exceeded in comicality by Justice Stareleigh's bewilderment a moment afterwards, upon her saying that she "see Mrs. Bardell's street-door on the jar."

JUDGE (in immense astonishment).—"On the what?"

COUNSEL.—"Partly open, my lord."

JUDGE (with more owl-like stolidity than ever).—"She *said* on the jar."

COUNSEL.—"It's all the same, my lord."

Then—blinking more quickly than before, with a furtive glance at witness, and a doubtful look of abstraction into space—the little Judge made a note of it.

As in Mrs. Cluppins' faintness there was a recognizable touch of Mrs. Crupp, when the spasms were engendering in the nankeen bosom of that exemplary female, so also in the maternal confidences volunteered by the same witness, there was an appreciable reminder of another lady who will be remembered as having been introduced at the Coroner's Inquest in Bleak House as "Anastasia Piper, gentlemen." Regarding that as a favourable opportunity for informing the court of her own domestic affairs, through the medium of a brief dissertation, Mrs. Cluppins was interrupted by the irascible Judge at the most interesting point in her revelations, when, having mentioned that she was already the mother of eight children, she added, that "she entertained confident expectations of presenting Mr. Cluppins with a ninth about that day six months"—whereupon the worthy lady was summarily hustled out of the witness-box.

Nathaniel Winkle, however, consoled us immediately. Don't we remember how, even before he could open his lips, he was completely disconcerted? Namely, when, bowing very respectfully to the little Judge, he had that complimentary proceeding acknowledged snappishly with, "Don't look at me, sir; look at the jury——" Mr. Winkle, in obedience to the mandate, meekly looking "at the place where he thought that the jury might be." Don't we remember also perfectly well how the worst possible construction was cast by implication beforehand upon his probable reply to the very first question put to him, namely, by the mere manner in which that first question was put? "Now, sir, have the goodness to let his lordship and the jury know what your name is, will you?" Mr. Skimpin, in propounding this inquiry, inclining his head on one side and listening with great sharpness for the answer, "as if to imply that he rather thought Mr. Winkle's natural taste for perjury would induce him to give some name which did not belong to him." Giving in, absurdly, his surname only; and being asked immediately afterwards, if possible still more absurdly, by the Judge, "Have you any Christian name, sir?" the witness, in the Reading, more naturally and yet more confusedly even it seemed than in the book, got that eminent functionary into a great bewilderment as to whether he (Mr. Winkle) were called

Nathaniel Daniel, or Daniel Nathaniel. Bewildered himself, in his turn, and that too almost hopelessly, came Mr. Winkle's reply, " No, my lord; only Nathaniel—not Daniel at all." Irascibly, the Judge's, " What did you tell me it was Daniel for, then, sir?" Shamefaced and yet irritably, "I didn't, my lord." "You did, sir!"—with great indignation, topped by this cogent reasoning,—" How could I have got Daniel on my notes, unless you told me so, sir?" Nothing at all was said about it in the Reading; but, again and again, Mr. Winkle, as there impersonated, while endeavouring to feign an easiness of manner, was made to assume, in his then state of confusion, "rather the air of a disconcerted pickpocket."

Better almost than Mr. Winkle himself, however, as an impersonation, was, in look, voice, manner, Mr. Skimpin, the junior barrister, under whose cheerful but ruthless interrogations that unfortunate gentleman was stretched upon the rack of examination. His (Mr. Skimpin's) cheery echoing—upon every occasion when it was at last extorted from his victim—of the latter's answer (followed instantly by his own taunts and insinuations), remains as vividly as anything at all about this Reading in our recollection. When at length Mr. Winkle, with no reluctance in the world, but only seemingly with reluctance, answers the inquiry as to whether he is a particular friend of Pickwick, " Yes, I am!"—" *Yes, you are!*" said Mr. Skimpin (audibly to the court, but as if it were only to himself). "And why couldn't you say that at once, sir? Perhaps you know the plaintiff, too—eh, Mr. Winkle?" "I don't know her; I've seen her!" "Oh, *you don't know her, but you've seen her?* Now have the goodness to tell the gentlemen of the jury what you mean by *that*, Mr. Winkle." As to how this unfortunate witness, after being driven to the confines of desperation, on being at last released, "rushed with delirious haste" to the hotel, "where he was discovered some hours after by the waiter, groaning in a hollow and dismal manner, with his head buried beneath the sofa cushions"—not a word was said in the Reading.

A flavour of the fun of Mrs. Sanders's evidence was given, but only a passing flavour of it, in reference to Mr. Sanders having, in the course of their correspondence, often called her duck, but never chops, nor yet tomato-sauce—he being particularly fond of ducks—though possibly, if he had been equally fond of chops and tomato-sauce, he might have called her that instead, as a term of affection.

The evidence of all, however, was that of Sam Weller, no less to the enjoyment of the Author, it was plain to see, than to that of his hearers. After old Weller's hoarse and guttural cry from the gallery, "Put it down a wee, my lord," in answer to the inquiry whether the immortal surname was to be spelt with a V. or a W.; Sam's quiet "I rayther suspect it was my father, my lord," came with irresistible effect from the Reader, as also did his recollection of something "wery partickler" having happened on the memorable morning, out of which had sprung the whole of this trial of Bardell *v.* Pickwick, namely, that he himself that day had "a reg'lar new fit out o' clothes." Beyond all the other Wellerisms, however, was Sam's overwhelmingly conclusive answer to counsel's inquiry in regard to his not having seen what occurred, though he himself, at the time, was in the passage, "Have you a pair of eyes, Mr. Weller?" "Yes, I *have* a pair of eyes; and that's just it. If they wos a pair o' patent double-million magnifying gas microscopes of hextra power, p'r'aps I might be able to see through two flights o' stairs and a deal door; but *bein'* only eyes, you see, my wision's limited." Better by far, in our estimation, nevertheless, than the smart Cockney facetiousness of the inimitable Sam; better than the old coachman's closing lamentation, "Vy worn't there a alleybi?" better than Mr. Winkle, or Mrs. Cluppins, or Serjeant Buzfuz, or than all the rest of those engaged in any capacity in the trial, put together, was the irascible little Judge, with the blinking eyes and the monotonous voice—himself, in his very *pose*, obviously, "all face and waistcoat." Than Mr. Justice Stareleigh there was, in the whole of this most humorous of all the Readings, no more highly comic impersonation.

DAVID COPPERFIELD.

The sea-beach at Yarmouth formed both the opening and the closing scene of this Reading, in six chapters, from "David Copperfield." In its varied portraiture of character and in the wonderful descriptive power marking its conclusion, it was one of the most interesting and impressive of the whole series in its delivery. Through it, we renewed our acquaintance more vividly than ever with handsome, curly-headed, reckless, heartless Steerforth! With poor, lone, lorn Mrs. Gummidge, not only when everythink about her went contrairy, but when her better nature gushed forth under the great calamity befalling her benefactor. With pretty little Emily, and bewitching little Dora. With Mr. Micawber, his shirt-collar, his eye-glass, the condescending roll in his voice, and his intermittent bursts of confidence. With Mrs. Micawber, who, as the highest praise we can bestow upon her, is quite worthy of her husband, and who is always, it will be remembered, so impassioned in her declaration that, come what may, she never *will* desert

Mr. Micawber! With Traddles, and his irrepressible hair, even a love-lock from which had to be kept down by Sophy's preservation of it in a clasped locket! With Mr. Peggotty, in fine, who, in his tender love for his niece, is, according to his own account, "not to look at, but to think on," nothing less than a babby in the form of a great sea Porkypine! Remembering the other originals, crowding the pages of the story in its integrity, how one would have liked to have seen even a few more of them impersonated by the protean Novelist! That "most wonderful woman in the world," Aunt Betsey, for example; or that most laconic of carriers, Mr. Barkis; or, to name yet one other, Uriah Heep, that reddest and most writhing of rascally attornies. As it was, however, there were abundant realizations within the narrow compass of this Reading of the principal persons introduced in the autobiography of David Copperfield. The most loveable, by the way, of all the young heroes portrayed in the Dickens' Gallery was there, to begin with, for example — the peculiar loveableness of David being indicated as plainly as by any means through the extraordinary variety of pet names given to him by one or another in the course of the narrative. For, was he not the "Daisy" of Steerforth, the "Doady" of Dora, the "Trotwood" of Aunt Betsy, and the "Mas'r Davy" of the Yarmouth boatmen, just as surely as he was the "Mr. Copperfull" of Mrs. Crupp, the "Master Copperfield" of

Uriah Heep, and the "Dear Copperfield" of Mr. Wilkins Micawber?

That "The Personal History and Experiences of David Copperfield the Younger" was, among all its author's works, his own particular favourite, he himself, in his very last preface to it, in 1867, formally acknowledged. Several years previously, while sauntering with him to and fro one evening on the grass-plot at Gadshill, we remember receiving from him that same admission. "Which of all your books do you think I regard as incomparably your best?" "Which?" "David Copperfield." A momentary pause ensuing, he added, readily and without the smallest reservation, "You are quite right." The acknowledgment then made as to this being in fact his own opinion was thus simply but emphatically expressed. Pen in hand, long afterwards, he made the same admission, only with yet greater emphasis, when the Preface to the new edition of the story in 1867 was thus closed by Charles Dickens—"Of all my books, I like this the best. It will be easily believed that I am a fond parent to every child of my fancy, and that no one can ever love that family as dearly as I love them. But, like many fond parents, I have in my heart of hearts a favourite child. And his name is 'David Copperfield.'" Having that confession from his own lips and under his own hand, it will be readily understood that the Novelist always took an especial delight when, in the course of his Readings, the turn came for that of "David Copperfield."

One of the keenest sensations of pleasure he ever experienced as a Reader—as he himself related to us with the liveliest gratification, evidently, even in the mere recollection of the incident—occurred in connection with this very Reading. Strange to say, moreover, it occurred, not in England or in America, in the presence of an English-speaking audience, but in Paris, and face to face with an audience more than half of which was composed of Frenchmen. And the hearer who caused him, there, that artistic sense, one might almost call it thrill of satisfaction—was a Frenchman! All that was expressed on the part of this appreciative listener, being uttered by him instantaneously in a half-whispered, monosyllabic ejaculation. As we have already explained upon an earlier page, the Readings which took place in Paris, and which were in behalf of the British Charitable Fund in that capital, were given there before a densely crowded but very select audience at the British Embassy, Lord Cowley being then her Majesty's ambassador. The Reading on the occasion referred to was "David Copperfield," and the Reader became aware in the midst of the hushed silence, just after he had been saying, in the voice of Steerforth, giving at the same moment a cordial grasp of the hand to the briny fisherman he was addressing: "Mr. Peggotty, you are a thoroughly good fellow, and deserve to be as happy as you are to-night. My hand upon it!" when, turning round, he added, still as Steerforth, but speaking in a very different voice and offering a very different hand-grip, as though already he were thinking to himself what a chuckle-headed fellow the young shipwright was—"Ham, I give you joy, my boy. My hand upon that too!" The always keenly observant Novelist became aware of a Frenchman, who was eagerly listening in the front row of the stalls, suddenly exclaiming to himself, under his breath, "Ah—h!"—having instantly caught the situation! The sound of that one inarticulate monosyllable, as he observed, when relating the circumstance, gave the Reader, as an artist, a far livelier sense of satisfaction than any that could possibly have been imparted by mere acclamations, no matter how spontaneous or enthusiastic.

As a Reading, it always seemed to us, that "David Copperfield" was cut down rather distressingly. That, nevertheless, was unavoidable. Turning in off Yarmouth sands, we went straight at once through the "delightful door" cut in its side, into the old black barge or boat, high and dry there on the sea-beach, and which was known to us nearly as familiarly as to David himself, as the odd dwelling-house inhabited by Mr. Peggotty. All the still-life of that beautifully clean and tidy interior we had revealed to us again, as of old: lockers, boxes, table, Dutch clock, chest of drawers—even tea-tray, only that we failed to hear anything said about the painting on the tea-tray, representing "a lady with a parasol, taking a walk with a military-looking child, who was trundling a hoop." The necessities of condensation in the same way restricted the definition of Mr. Peggotty's occupation in the Reading, to the simple mention of the fact that he dealt in lobsters, crabs, and craw-fish, without any explanation at all as to those creatures being heaped together in a little wooden out-house "in a state of wonderful conglomeration with one another, and never leaving off pinching whatever they laid hold of." Little Emily appeared as a beautiful young woman, and no longer as the prattling lassie who, years before had confided to her playfellow, David, how, if ever she were a lady, she would give uncle Dan, meaning Mr. Peggotty, "a sky-blue coat, with diamond buttons, nankeen trousers, a red velvet waistcoat, a cocked hat, a large gold watch, a silver pipe, and a box of money." Mrs. Gummidge, as became a faithful widow, was still fretting after the Old 'Un. Ham, something of Mr. Peggotty's own build, as the latter described him, "a good deal o' the sou-wester in him, wery salt, but on the whole, a honest sort of a chap, too, with his 'art in the right place," had just made good his betrothal to the little creature he had seen grow up there before him, "like a flower," when, at the very opening of the Reading, into the old Yarmouth boat, walked "Mas'r Davy" and his friend Steerforth. Mr. Peggotty's explanation to his unexpected but heartily welcomed visitors as to how the engagement between Ham and Emily, had but just then been brought about, opened up before the audience in a few words the whole scheme of the tragic little dramatic tale about to be revealed to them through a series of vivid impersonations.

The idiomatic sentences of the bluff fisherman, as in their racy vernacular they were blithely given utterance to by the manly voice of the Reader, seemed to supply a fitting introduction to the drama, as though from the lips of a Yarmouth Chorus. Scarcely had the social carouse there in the old boat, on that memorable evening of Steerforth's introduction, been recounted, when the whole drift of the story was clearly foreshadowed in the brief talk which immediately took place between him and David as they walked townwards across the sands towards their hotel. "Daisy,—for though that's not the name your godfathers and godmothers gave you, you're such a fresh fellow, that it's the name I best like to call you by—and I wish, I wish, I wish you could give it to me!" That of itself had its significance. But still more significant was David's mention of his looking in at Steerforth's bed-room on the following morning, before himself going away alone, and of his there finding the handsome scapegrace fast asleep, "lying easily, with his head upon his arm," as he had often seen him lie in the old school dormitory. "Thus in this silent hour I left him," with mournful tenderness, exclaimed the Reader, in the words and accents of his young hero. "Never more, O God forgive you, Steerforth! to touch that passive hand in love and friendship. Never, never more!" The revelation of his treachery, towards the pretty little betrothed of the young shipwright, followed immediately afterwards, on the occasion of David's next visit, some months later, to the old boat on the flats at Yarmouth.

The wonder still is to us, now that we are recalling to mind the salient peculiarities of this Reading, as we do so, turning over leaf by leaf the marked copy of it, from which the Novelist read; the wonder, we repeat, still is to us how, in that exquisite scene, the very words that have always moved us most in the novel were struck out in the delivery, are rigidly scored through here with blue inkmarks in the reading copy, by the hand of the Reader-Novelist. Those words we mean which occur, where Ham, having on his arrival, made a movement as if Em'ly were outside, asked Mas'r Davy to "come out a minute," only for him, on his doing so, to find that Em'ly was not there, and that Ham was deadly pale. "Ham! what's the matter?" was gasped out in the Reading. But—*not* what follows, immediately on that, in the original narrative: "'Mas'r Davy!' Oh, for his broken heart, how dreadfully he wept!" Nor yet the sympathetic exclamations of David, who, in the novel, describes himself as paralysed by the sight of such grief, not knowing what he thought or what he dreaded; only able to look at him,

—yet crying out to him the next moment, "Ham! Poor, good fellow! For heaven's sake tell me what's the matter?" Nothing of this: only—"My love, Mas'r Davy—the pride and hope of my 'art, her that I'd have died for, and would die for now—she's gone!" "Gone?" "Em'ly's run away!" Ham, *not* then adding in the Reading, "Oh, Mas'r Davy, think *how* she's run away, when I pray my good and gracious God to kill her (her that is so dear above all things) sooner than let her come to ruin and disgrace!" Yet, for all that, in spite of these omissions—it can hardly by any chance have been actually by reason of them—the delivery of the whole scene was singularly powerful and affecting. Especially in the representation of Mr. Peggotty's profound grief, under what is to him so appalling a calamity. Especially also in the revelation of Mrs. Gummidge's pity for him, her gratitude to him, and her womanly tender-heartedness.

In charming relief to the sequel of this tragic incident of the bereavement of the Peggottys, came David's love passages with Dora, and his social unbendings with Mr. Micawber. Regaling the latter inimitable personage, and his equally inimitable wife, together with David's old schoolfellow, Traddles, on a banquet of boiled leg of mutton, very red inside and very pale outside, as well as upon a delusive pigeon-pie, the crust of which was like a disappointing phrenological head, "full of lumps and bumps, with nothing particular underneath," David afforded us the opportunity of realising, within a very brief interval, something at least of the abundant humour associated with Mrs. Micawber's worldly wisdom, and Mr. Micawber's ostentatious impecuniosity. A word, that last, it always seems to us—describing poverty, as it does, with such an air of pomp—especially provided beforehand for Mr. Micawber (out of a prophetic anticipation or foreknowledge of him) by the dictionary.

The mere opening of the evening's entertainment at David Copperfield's chambers on this occasion, enabled the Humorist to elicit preliminary roars of laughter from his audience by his very manner of saying, with a deliciously ridiculous prolongation of the liquid consonant forming the initial of the last word—"As to Mrs. Micawber, I don't know whether it was the effect of the cap, or the lavender water, or the pins, or the fire, or the wax-candles, but she came out of my room comparatively speaking l-l-lovely!"

As deliciously ridiculous was the whole scene between Dora and David, where the latter, at length, takes courage to make his proposal—"Jip barking madly all the time"—Dora crying the while and trembling. David's eloquence increasing, the more he raved, the more Jip barked—each, in his own way, getting more mad every moment! Even when they had got married by licence, "the Archbishop of Canterbury invoking a blessing, and doing it as cheap as it could possibly be expected," their domestic experiences were sources of unbounded merriment.

As, for example, in connection with their servant girl's cousin in the Life Guards, "with such long legs that he looked like the afternoon shadow of somebody else." Finally, closing the whole of this ingenious epitome of the original narrative, came that grand and wonderfully realistic description of the stupendous storm upon the beach at Yarmouth, upon the extraordinary power of which as a piece of declamation we have already at some length commented. There, in the midst of the dying horrors of that storm—there, on those familiar sands, where Mas'r Davy and Little Em'ly had so often looked for shells when they were children, on the very spot where some lighter fragments of the old boat, blown down the night before, had been scattered by the tempest, David Copperfield was heard describing, in the last mournful sentence of the Reading, how he saw *him* lying with his curly head upon his arm, as he had often seen him lie when they were at school together.

THE CRICKET ON THE HEARTH.

A Fairy Tale of Home was here related, that in its graceful and fantastic freaks of fancy might have been imagined by the Danish poet, Hans Christian Andersen. In its combination of simple pathos and genial drollery, however, it was a story that no other could by possibility have told than the great English Humorist. If there was something really akin to the genius of Andersen, in the notion of the Cricket with its shrill, sharp, piercing voice resounding through the house, and seeming to twinkle in the outer darkness like a star, Dickens, and no other could, by any chance, have conjured up the forms of either Caleb Plummer, or Gruff-and-Tackleton. The cuckoo on the Dutch clock, now like a spectral voice, now hiccoughing on the assembled company, as if he had got drunk for joy; the little haymaker over the dial mowing down imaginary grass, jerking right and left with his scythe in front of a Moorish palace; the hideous, hairy, red-eyed jacks-in-boxes; the flies in the Noah's arks, that "an't on that scale neither as compared with elephants;" the giant masks, having a certain furtive leer, " safe to destroy the peace of mind of any young gentlemen between the ages of six and eleven, for the whole Christmas or Midsummer vacation," were all of them like dreams of the Danish poet, coloured into a semblance of life by the grotesque humour of the English Novelist. But dear little Dot, who was rather of the dumpling's shape—" but I don't myself object to that "—and good, lumbering John Peerybingle, her husband, often so near to something or another very clever, according to his own account, and Boxer, the carrier's dog, " with that preposterous nothing of a fag-end of a tail of his, describing circles of barks round the horse, making savage rushes at his mistress, and facetiously bringing himself to sudden stops,"—all bear upon them unmistakably the sign-manual of Boz.

As originally recounted in the Christmas story-book, the whole narrative was comprised within a very few pages, portioned out into three little chirps. Yet the letter-press was illustrated profusely by pencils as eminent as those of Daniel Maclise, of Clarkson Stanfield, of Richard Doyle, of John Leech, of Sir Edwin Landseer. The charming little fairy tale, moreover, was inscribed to Lord Jeffrey. It was a favourite of his, as it still is of many another critic north and south of the Tweed, light, nay trivial, though the materials out of which the homely apologue is composed. It can hardly be wondered at, however, remembering how less than four years prior to its first publication, a literary reviewer, no less formidable than Professor

Wilson—while abstaining, in his then capacity as chairman of the public banquet given to Charles Dickens at Edinburgh, from attempting, as he said, anything like "a critical delineation of our illustrious guest"—nevertheless, added emphatically, "I cannot but express in a few ineffectual words the delight which every human bosom feels in the benign spirit which pervades all his creations." Christopher North thus further expressed his admiration then of the young English Novelist—"How kind and good a man he is," the great Critic exclaimed, laying aside for a while the crutch with which he had so often, in the Ambrosian Nights, brained many an arrant pretender to the title of genius or of philanthropist, and turning his lion-like eyes, at the moment beaming only with cordiality, on the then youthful face of Dickens,—"How kind and good a man he is I need not say, nor what strength of genius he has acquired by that profound sympathy with his fellow-creatures, whether in prosperity and happiness, or overwhelmed with unfortunate circumstances."

Purely and simply, in his capacity as an imaginative writer, the Novelist had already (then in the June of 1841) impressed thus powerfully the heart and judgment of John Wilson, of Christopher North, of the inexorable Rhadamanthus of *Blackwood* and the "Noctes." Afterwards, but a very little more than two years afterwards, came the "Carol." The following winter rang out the "Chimes." The Christmas after that was heard the chirping of the "Cricket."

Four years previously Professor Wilson, on the occasion referred to, had remarked of him most truly,—"He has not been deterred by the aspect of vice and wickedness, and misery and guilt, from seeking a spirit of good in things evil, but has endeavoured by the might of genius to transmute what was base into what is precious as the beaten gold;" observing, indeed, yet further—"He has mingled in the common walks of life; he has made himself familiar with the lower orders of society." As if in supplementary and conclusive justification of those words, Dickens, within less than five years afterwards, had woven his graceful and pathetic fancies about the homely joys and sorrows of Bob Cratchit, of Toby Veck, and of Caleb Plummer, of a little Clerk, a little Ticket-porter, and a little Toy-maker. His pen at these times was like the wand of Cinderella's fairy godmother, changing the cucumber into a gilded chariot, and the lizards into glittering retainers.

At the commencement of this Reading but very little indeed was said about the Cricket, hardly anything at all about the kettle. Yet, as everybody knows, "the kettle began it" in the story-book. The same right of precedence was accorded to the kettle in the author's delivery of his fairy tale by word of mouth, but otherwise its comfortable purring song was in a manner hushed. One heard nothing about its first appearance on the hearth, when "it *would* lean forward with a drunken air, and dribble, a very idiot of a kettle," any more than of its final pæan, when, after its iron body hummed and stirred upon the fire, the lid itself, the recently rebellious lid, performed a sort of jig, and clattered "like a deaf and dumb young cymbal that had never known the use of its twin brother." Here, again, in fact, as with so many other of these Readings from his own books by our Novelist, the countless good things scattered abundantly up and down the original descriptions—inimitable touches of humour that had each of them, on the appreciative palate, the effect of that verbal bon-bon, the bon-mot—were sacrificed inexorably, apparently without a qualm, and certainly by wholesale. What the Reader looked to throughout, was the human element in his imaginings when they were to be impersonated.

Let but one of these tid-bits be associated directly with the fanciful beings introduced in the gradual unfolding of the incidents, and it might remain there untouched. Thus, for example, when the Carrier's arrival at his home came to be mentioned, and the Reader related how John Peerybingle, being much taller, as well as much older than his wife, little Dot, "had to stoop a long way down to kiss her"—the words that followed thereupon were happily *not* omitted: "but she was worth the trouble,—*six foot six with the lumbago might have done it.*" Several of John's choicest—all-but jokes were also retained. As, where Dot is objecting to be called by that pet diminutive, "'Why, what else are you?' returned John, looking down upon her with a smile, and giving her waist as light a squeeze as his huge hand and arm could give, 'A dot and'—here he glanced at the baby—'a dot and carry'—I won't say it, for fear I should spoil it; but I was very near a joke. I don't know as ever I was nearer." Tilly Slowboy and her charge, the baby, were, upon every mention of them in the Reading, provocative of abundant laughter. The earliest allusion to Miss Slowboy recording these characteristic circumstances in regard to her costume, that it "was remarkable for the partial development, on all possible and impossible occasions, of some flannel vestment of a singular structure, also for affording glimpses in the region of the back of a pair of stays, in colour a dead green." On the introduction of the Mysterious Stranger—apparently all but stone deaf—from the Carrier's cart, where he had been forgotten, the comic influence of the Reading became irresistible.

STRANGER (on noticing Dot) interrogatively to John.—"Your Daughter?"

CARRIER, with the voice of a boatswain.—"Wife."

STRANGER, with his hand to his ear, being not quite certain that he has caught it.—"Niece?"

CARRIER, with a roar.—"Wife."

Satisfied at last upon that point, the stranger asks of John, as a new matter of curiosity to him, "Baby, yours?" Whereupon the Reader, *as* John, "gave a gigantic nod, equivalent to an answer in the affirmative, delivered through a speaking-trumpet." Stranger, still unsatisfied, inquiring,—"Girl?"—"Bo-o-oy!" was bellowed back by John Peerybingle. It was when Mrs. Peerybingle herself took up the parable, however, that the merriment excited among the audience became fairly irrepressible. Scarcely had the nearly stone-deaf stranger added, in regard to the "Bo-o-oy,"—"Also very young, eh?" (a comment previously applied by him to Dot) when the Reader, as Mrs. Peerybingle, instantly struck in, at the highest pitch of his voice, that is, of *her* voice (the comic effect of this being simply indescribable)—"Two months and three da-ays! Vaccinated six weeks ago-o! Took very fine-ly! Considered, by the doctor, a remarkably beautiful chi-ild! Equal to the general run of children at five months o-old! Takes notice in a way quite won-der-ful! May seem impossible to *you*, but feels his feet al-ready!"

Directly afterwards, Caleb Plummer appeared upon the scene, little imagining that in the Mysterious Stranger would be discovered, later on, under the disguise of that nearly stone-deaf old gentleman, his (Caleb's) own dear boy, Edward, supposed to have died in the golden South Americas. Little Caleb's inquiry of Mrs. Peerybingle,—"You couldn't have the goodness to let me pinch Boxer's tail, Mum, for half a moment, could you?" was one of the welcome whimsicalities of the Reading. "Why, Caleb! what a question!" naturally enough was Dot's instant exclamation. "Oh, never mind, Mum!" said the little toy-maker, apologetically, "He mightn't like it perhaps"—adding, by way of explanation—" There's a small order just come in, for barking dogs; and I should wish to go as close to Natur' as I could, for sixpence!" Caleb's employer, Tackleton, in his large green cape and bull-headed looking mahogany tops, was then described as entering pretty much in the manner of what one might suppose to be that of an ogrish toy-merchant. His character came out best perhaps—meaning, in another sense, that is, at its worst—when the fairy spirit of John's house, the Cricket, was heard chirping; and Tackleton asked, grumpily,—"Why don't you kill that cricket? *I* would! I always do! I hate their noise!" John exclaiming, in amazement,—"You kill your crickets, eh?" "*Scrunch 'em*, sir!" quoth Tackleton.

One of the most wistfully curious thoughts uttered in the whole of the Reading was the allusion to the original founder of the toy-shop of Gruff and Tackleton, where it was remarked (such a quaint epitome of human life!) that under that same crazy roof, beneath which Caleb Plummer and Bertha, his blind daughter, found shelter as their humble home,—" the Gruff before last had, in a small way, *made toys for a generation of old boys and girls, who had played with them, and found them out, and broken them, and gone to sleep*." Another wonderfully comic minor character was introduced later on in the eminently ridiculous person of old Mrs. Fielding—in regard to in-door gloves, a foreshadowing of Mrs. Wilfer—in the matter of her imaginary losses through the indigo trade, a spectral precursor, or dim prototype, as one might say, of Mrs. Pipchin and the Peruvian mines. Throughout the chief part of the dreamy, dramatic little story, the various characters, it will be remembered, are involved in a mazy entanglement of cross purposes. Mystery sometimes, pathos often, terror for one brief interval, rose from the Reading of the "Home Fairy-Tale." There was a subdued tenderness which there was no resisting in the revelation to the blind girl, Bertha, of the illusions in which she had been lapped for years by her sorcerer of a father, poor little Caleb, the toy-maker. There was at once a tearful and a laughing earnestness that took the Reader's audience captive, not by any means unwillingly, when little Dot was, at the last, represented as "clearing it all up at home" (indirectly, to the great honour of the Cricket's reputation, by the way) to her burly husband—good, stupid, worthy, "clumsy man in general,"—John Peerybingle, the Carrier. The one inconsistent person in the whole story, it must be admitted, was Tackleton, who turned out at the very end to be rather a good fellow than otherwise. Fittingly enough, in the Reading as in the book, when the "Fairy Tale of Home" was related to its close, when Dot and all the rest were spoken of as vanished, a broken child's-toy, we were told, yet lay upon the ground, and still upon the hearth was heard the song of the Cricket.

NICHOLAS NICKLEBY.

A VARIETY of attractive Readings might readily have been culled from Nicholas Nickleby's Life and Adventures. His comical experiences as a strolling-player in the Company of the immortal Crummleses—his desperate encounter with Sir Mulberry Hawk on the footboard of the cabriolet—his exciting rescue of Madeline from an unholy alliance with Gride, the miser, on the very morning fixed for the revolting marriage—his grotesque association for a while with the Kenwigses and their uncle Lillivick—his cordial relations with the Brothers Cheeryble and old Tim Linkinwater—any one of these incidents in the career of the most high spirited of all the young heroes of our Novelist, would have far more than simply justified its selection as the theme of one of these illustrative entertainments. Instead of choosing any one of those later episodes in the fictitious history of Nicholas Nickleby, however, the author of that enthralling romance of everyday life, picked out, by preference, the earliest of all his young hero's experiences—those in which, at nineteen years of age, he was brought into temporary entanglement with the domestic economy of Dotheboys Hall, and at the last into personal conflict with its one-eyed principal, the rascally Yorkshire school-master.

The Gadshill collection of thin octavos, comprising the whole series of Readings, includes within it two copies of "Mrs. Gamp" and two copies of "Nicholas Nickleby." Whereas, on comparing the duplicates of Mrs. Gamp, the two versions appear to be so slightly different that they are all but identical, a marked contrast is observable at a glance between the two Nicklebys. Each Reading is descriptive, it is true, of his sayings and doings at the Yorkshire school. But, even externally, one of the two copies is marked "Short Time,"—the love-passages with Miss Squeers being entirely struck out, and no mention whatever being made of John Browdie, the corn-factor. The wretched school, the sordid rascal who keeps it, Mrs. Squeers, poor, forlorn Smike, and a few of his scarecrow companions—these, in the short-time version, and these alone, constitute the young usher's surroundings. In here recalling to recollection the "Nicholas Nickleby" Reading at all, however, we select, as a matter of course, the completer version, the one for which the generality of hearers had an evident preference: the abbreviated version being always regarded as capital, so far as it went; but even at the best, with all the go and dash of its rapid delivery, insufficient.

Everything, even, we should imagine, to one unacquainted with the novel, was ingeniously explained by the Reader in a sentence or two at starting. Nicholas Nickleby was described as arriving early one November morning, at the Saracen's Head, to join, in his new capacity (stripling though he was) as scholastic assistant, Mr. Squeers, "the cheap—the terribly cheap" Yorkshire schoolmaster. The words just given in inverted commas are those written in blue ink in the Novelist's handwriting on the margin of his longer Reading copy. As also are the following words, epitomising in a breath the position of the young hero when the story commences—"Inexperienced, sanguine, and thrown upon the world with no adviser, and his bread to win," the manuscript interpolation thus intimates: the letterpress then relating in its integrity that Nicholas had engaged himself as tutor at Mr. Wackford Squeers's academy, on the strength of the memorable advertisement in the London newspapers. The advertisement, that is, comprising within it the long series of accomplishments imparted to the students at Dotheboys Hall, including "single-stick" (if required), together with "fortification, and every other branch of classical literature." The Reader laying particular stress, among other items in the announcement, upon "No extras, no vacations, and diet unparalleled;" and upon the finishing touch (having especial reference to the subject in hand), "An able assistant wanted: annual salary, £5! A master of arts would be preferred!" Immediately after this, in the Reading, came the description of Mr. Squeers, several of the particulars in regard to whose villainous appearance always told wonderfully: as, where it was said "he had but one eye, and the popular prejudice runs in favour of two;" or, again, where in reference to his attire—it having been mentioned that his coat-sleeves were a great deal too long and his trousers a great deal too short—it was added that "he appeared ill at ease in his clothes, and as if he were in a perpetual state of astonishment at finding himself so respectable." Listening to the Reader, we were there, in the coffee-room of the Saracen's Head—the rascal Squeers in the full enjoyment of his repast of hot toast and cold round of beef, the while five little boys sat opposite hungrily and thirstily expectant of their share in a miserable meal of two-penn'orth of milk and thick bread and butter for three. "Just fill that mug up with lukewarm water, William, will you?" "To the wery top, sir? Why the milk will be drownded!" "*Serve it right for being so dear!*" Squeers adding with a chuckle, as he pounded away at his own coffee and viands,—"Conquer your passions, boys, and don't be eager after wittles." To see the Reader as Squeers, stirring the mug of lukewarm milk and water, and then smacking his lips with an affected relish after tasting a spoonful of it, before reverting to his own fare of buttered toast and beef, was to be there with Nicholas, a spectator on that wintry morning in the Snow Hill

Tavern, watching the guttling pedagogue and the five little famished expectants. Only when Squeers, immediately before the signal for the coach starting, wiped his mouth, with a self-satisfied "Thank God for a good breakfast," was the mug rapidly passed from mouth to mouth at once ravenously and tantalizingly.

The long and bitter journey on the north road, through the snow, was barely referred to in the Reading; due mention, however, being made, and always tellingly, of Mr. Squeers's habit of getting down at nearly every stage—"to stretch his legs, he said,—and as he always came back with a very red nose, and composed himself to sleep directly, the stretching seemed to answer." Immediately on the wayfarers' arrival at Dotheboys, Mrs. Squeers, arrayed in a dimity night-jacket, herself a head taller than Mr. Squeers, was always introduced with great effect, as seizing her Squeery by the throat and giving him two loud kisses in rapid succession, like a postman's knock. The audience then scarcely had time to laugh over the interchange of questions and answers between the happy couple, as to the condition of the cows and pigs, and, last of all, the boys, ending with Madame's intimation that "young Pitcher's had a fever," followed up by Squeers's characteristic exclamation, "No! damn that chap, he's always at something of that sort"—when there came the first glimpse of poor Smike, in a skeleton suit, and large boots originally made for tops, too patched and ragged now for a beggar; around his throat "a tattered child's frill only half concealed by a coarse man's neckerchief." Anxiously observing Squeers, as he emptied his overcoat of letters and papers, the boy did this, we were told, with an air so dispirited and hopeless, that Nicholas could hardly bear to watch him. "Have you—did anybody—has nothing been heard—about me?" were then (in the faintest, frightened voice!) the first stammered utterances of the wretched drudge. Bullied into silence by the brutal schoolmaster, Smike limped away with a vacant smile, when we heard the female scoundrel in the dimity night-jacket saying,—"I'll tell you what, Squeers, I think that young chap's turning silly."

Inducted into the loathsome school-room on the following morning by Squeers himself, Nicholas, first of all, we were informed, witnessed the manner in which that arrant rogue presided over "the first class in English spelling and philosophy," practically illustrating his mode of tuition by setting the scholars to clean the w-i-n win, d-e-r-s ders, winders—to weed the garden—to rub down the horse, or get rubbed down themselves if they didn't do it well. Nicholas assisted in the afternoon, moreover, at the report given by Mr. Squeers on his return homewards after his half-yearly visit to the metropolis. Beginning, though this last-mentioned part of the Reading did, with Squeers's ferocious slash on the desk with his cane, and his announcement, in the midst of a death-like silence

"Let any boy speak a word without leave, and I'll take the skin off that boy's back!" many of the particulars given immediately afterwards by the Reader were, in spite of the surrounding misery, irresistibly provocative of laughter. Ample justification for this, in truth, is very readily adduceable. Mr. Squeers having, through his one eye, made a mental abstract of Cobbey's letter, for example, Cobbey and the whole school were thus feelingly informed of its contents—"Oh! Cobbey's grandmother is dead, and his uncle John has took to drinking. Which is all the news his sister sends, except eighteen-pence—which will just pay for that broken square of glass! Mrs. Squeers, my dear, will you take the money?" Another while, Graymarsh's maternal aunt, who "thinks Mrs. Squeers must be a angel," and that Mr. Squeers is too good for this world, "would have sent the two pairs of stockings, as desired, but is short of money, so forwards a tract instead," and so on; "Ah! a delightful letter—very affecting, indeed!" quoth Squeers. "It was affecting in one sense!" observed the Reader; "for Graymarsh's maternal aunt was strongly supposed by her more intimate friends to be his maternal parent!"

Perhaps the epistle from Mobbs's mother-in-law was the best of all, however—the old lady who "took to her bed on hearing that he wouldn't eat fat;" and who "wishes to know by an early post where he expects to go to, if he quarrels with his vittles?" adding, "This was told her in the London newspapers—not by Mr.

Squeers, for he is too kind and too good to set anybody against anybody!"

As an interlude, overflowing with fun, came Miss Squeers's tea-drinking—the result of her suddenly falling in love with the new usher, and that chiefly by reason of the straightness of his legs, "the general run of legs at Dotheboys Hall being crooked." How John Browdie (with his hair damp from washing) appeared upon the occasion in a clean shirt—"whereof the collars might have belonged to some giant ancestor,"—and greeted the assembled company, including his intended, Tilda Price, "with a grin that even the collars could not conceal," the creator of the worthy Yorkshireman went on to describe, with a gusto akin to the relish with which every utterance of John Browdie's was caught up by the listeners. Whether he spoke in good humour or in ill humour, the burly cornfactor was equally delightful. One while saying, laughingly, to Nicholas, across the bread-and-butter plate which they had just been emptying between them, "Ye wean't get bread-and-butther ev'ry neight, I expect, mun. Ecod, they dean't put too much intif 'em. Ye'll be nowt but skeen and boans if you stop here long eneaf. Ho! ho! ho!"—all this to Nicholas's unspeakable indignation. Or, another while, after chafing in jealousy for a long time over the coquetries going on between Tilda Price and Nicholas—the Yorkshireman flattening his own nose with his clenched fist again and again, "as if to keep his hand in till he had an opportunity of exercising it on the nose of some other gentleman,"—until asked merrily by his betrothed to keep his glum silence no longer, but to say something: "Say summat?" roared John Browdie, with a mighty blow on the table; "Weal, then! what I say 's this—Dang my boans and boddy, if I stan' this ony longer! Do ye gang whoam wi' me; and do yon loight and toight young whipster look sharp out for a brokken head next time he cums under my hond. Cum whoam, tell'e, cum whoam!" After Smike's running away, and his being brought back again, had been rapidly recounted, what nearly every individual member of every audience in attendance at this Reading was eagerly on the watch for all along, at last, in the fullness of time, arrived,—the execrable Squeers receiving, instead of administering, a frightful beating, in the presence of the whole school; having carefully provided himself beforehand, as all were rejoiced to remember, with "a fearful instrument of flagellation, strong, supple, wax-ended, and new!"

So real are the characters described by Charles Dickens in his life-like fictions, and so exactly do the incidents he relates as having befallen them resemble actual occurrences, that we recall to recollection at this moment the delight with which the late accomplished Lady Napier once related an exact case in point, appealing, as she did so, to her husband, the author of the "Peninsular War," to corroborate the accuracy of her retrospect! Telling how she perfectly well remembered, when the fourth green number of "Nicholas Nickleby" was just out, one of her home group, who had a moment before caught sight of the picture of the flogging in a shop-window, rushed in with the startling announcement—as though he were bringing with him the news of some great victory—"What DO you think? *Nicholas has thrashed Squeers!*"

As the Novelist read this chapter, or rather the condensation of this chapter, it was for all the world like assisting in person at that sacred and refreshing rite!

"Is every boy here?"

Yes, every boy was there, and so was every observant listener, in eager and—knowing what was coming—in delighted expectation. As Squeers was represented as "glaring along the lines," to assure himself that every boy really *was* there, what time "every eye drooped and every head cowered down," the Reader, instead of uttering one word of what the ruffianly schoolmaster ought then to have added: "Each boy keep to his place. Nickleby! you go to your desk, sir!"—instead of saying one syllable of this, contented himself with obeying his own manuscript marginal direction, in one word—POINTING! The effect of this simple gesture was startling—particularly when, after the momentary hush with which it was always accompanied, he observed quietly,—"There was a curious expression in the usher's face, but he took his seat without opening his lips in reply." Then, when the schoolmaster had dragged in the wretched Smike by the collar, "or rather by that fragment of his jacket which was nearest the place where his collar ought to have been," there was a horrible relish in his saying, over his shoulder for a moment, "Stand a little out of the way, Mrs. Squeers, my dear; *I've hardly got room enough!*" The instant one cruel blow had fallen—"STOP!" was cried in a voice that made the rafters ring—even the lofty rafters of St. James's Hall.

SQUEERS, with the glare and snarl of a wild beast.—"Who cried stop?"

NICHOLAS.—"I did! This must not go on!"

SQUEERS, again, with a frightful look.—"Must not go on?"

NICHOLAS.—"Must not! Shall not! I will prevent it!"

Then came Nicholas Nickleby's manly denunciation of the scoundrel, interrupted one while for an instant by Squeers screaming out, "Sit down, you—beggar!" and followed at its close by the last and crowning outrage, consequent on a violent outbreak of wrath on the part of Squeers, who spat at him and struck him a blow across the face with his instrument of torture: when Nicholas, springing upon him, wrested the weapon from his hand, and pinning him by the throat—don't we all exult in the remembrance of it?—"beat the ruffian till he roared for mercy."

After that climax has been attained, two other particulars are alone worthy of being recalled to recollection in regard to this Reading. First, the indescribable heartiness of John Browdie's cordial shake-of-the-hand with Nicholas Nickleby on their encountering each other by accident upon the high road. "Shake honds? Ah! that I weel!" coupled with his ecstatic shout (so ecstatic that his horse shyed at it), "Beatten schoolmeasther! Ho! ho! ho! Beatten schoolmeasther! Who ever heard o' the loike o' that, noo? Give us thee hond agean, yoongster! Beatten schoolmeasther! Dang it, I loove thee for 't!" Finally, and as the perfecting touch of tenderness between the two cousins, then unknown to each other as such, in the early morning light at Boroughbridge, we caught a glimpse of Nicholas and Smike passing, hand in hand, out of the old barn together.

MR. BOB SAWYER'S PARTY.

Quite as exhilarating in its way as the all-but dramatised report of the great breach of promise case tried before Mr. Justice Stareleigh, was that other condensation of a chapter from "Pickwick," descriptive of Mr. Bob Sawyer's Party. It was a Reading, in the delivery of which the Reader himself had evidently the keenest sense of enjoyment. As a humorous description, it was effervescent with fun, being written throughout in the happiest, earliest style of the youthful genius of Boz, when the green numbers were first shaking the sides of lettered and unlettered Englishmen alike with Homeric laughter. Besides this, when given by him as a Reading, it comprised within it one of his very drollest impersonations. If only as the means of introducing us to Jack Hopkins, it would have been most acceptable. But, inimitable though Jack was, he was, at the least, thoroughly well companioned.

As a relish of what was coming, there was that preliminary account of the locality in which the festivities were held, to wit, Lant Street, in the borough large black wooden beads. Child being fond of toys, cribbed necklace, hid, played with cut string, and swallowed a bead. Child thought it capital fun, went back next day, and swallowed another bead."

Bless my heart what a dreadful thing! I beg your pardon, sir. Go on.

"Next day, child swallowed two beads; the day after that, treated himself to three so on, till in a week's time he had got through the necklace—five-and-twenty beads sister industrious girl, seldom treated herself to bit of finery cried eyes out, at loss of necklace; looked high and low for it but, I needn't say, didn't find few days afterwards, family at dinner—baked shoulder of mutton, and potatoes child, wasn't hungry, playing about the room, when suddenly there was heard a devil of a noise, like small hail storm. 'Don't do that, my boy,' said father. 'I aint a doin' nothing'

of Southwark, the prevailing repose of which, we were told, "sheds a gentle melancholy upon the soul"—fully justifying its selection as a haven of rest by any one who wished "to abstract himself from the world, to remove himself from the reach of temptation, to place himself beyond the possibility of any inducement to look out of window!" As specimens of animated nature, familiarly met with in the neighbourhood, "the pot-boy, the muffin youth, and the baked potato man," had about them a perennial freshness. Whenever we were reminded, again, in regard to the principal characteristics of the population that it was migratory, "usually disappearing on the verge of quarter-day, and generally by night," her Majesty's revenues being seldom collected in that happy valley, its rents being pronounced dubious, and its water communication described as "frequently cut off," we found in respect to the whole picture thus lightly-sketched in, that age did not wither nor custom stale its infinite comicality.

It was when the familiar personages of the story were, one after another, introduced upon the scene, however, that the broad Pickwickian humour of it all began in earnest to be realised. After we had listened with chuckling enjoyment to the ludicrously minute account given of the elaborate preparations made for the reception of the visitors, even in the approaches to Mr. Bob Sawyer's apartment, down to the mention of the kitchen candle with a long snuff, that "burnt cheerfully on the ledge of the staircase window," we had graphically rendered the memorable scene between poor, dejected Bob and his little spitfire of a landlady, Mrs. Raddle. *So* dejected and generally suppressed was Bob in the Reading, however, that we should hardly have recognised that very archetype of the whole *genus* of rollicking Medical Students, as originally described in the pages of Pickwick, where he is depicted as attired in "a coarse blue coat, which, without being either a great-coat or a surtout, partook of the nature and qualities of both," having about him that sort of slovenly smartness and swaggering gait peculiar to young gentlemen who smoke in the streets by day, and shout and scream in the same by night, calling waiters by their Christian names, and altogether bearing a resemblance upon the whole to something like a dissipated Robinson Crusoe. Habited, Bob still doubtless was, in the plaid trousers and the large, rough coat and double-breasted waistcoat, but as for the "swaggering gait" just mentioned not a vestige of it remained. Nor could that be wondered at, indeed, for an instant, beholding and hearing, as we did, the shrill ferocity with which Mrs. Raddle had it out with him about the rent immediately before the arrival of his guests.

It is one of the distinctive peculiarities of Charles Dickens as a humorous Novelist, that the cream or quintessence of a jest is very often given by him quite casually in a parenthesis. It was equally distinctive of his peculiarities as a Reader, that the especial charm of his drollery was often conveyed by the merest aside. Thus it was with him in reference to Mrs. Raddle's "confounded little bill," when—in between Ben Allen's inquiry, "How long has it been running?" and Bob Sawyer's reply, "Only about a quarter and a month or so"—the Reader parenthetically remarked, with a philosophic air, "A bill, by the way, is the most extraordinary locomotive engine that the genius of man ever produced: it would keep on running during the longest lifetime without ever once stopping of its own accord." Thus also was it, when he added meditatively to Bob's hesitating explanation to Mrs. Raddle, "the fact is that I have been disappointed in the City to-day"—"Extraordinary place that City: astonishing number of men always *are* getting disappointed there." Hereupon it was that that fiercest of little women, Mrs. Raddle, who had entered "in a tremble with passion and pale with rage," fairly let out at her lodger. Her incidental bout with Mr. Ben Allen, when he soothingly (!) interpolated, "My good soul," was, in the Reading, in two senses, a memorable diversion. Beginning with a sarcastic quivering in her voice, "I am not *aweer*, sir, that you have any right to address your conversation to *me*. I don't think I let these apartments to *you*, sir—" Mrs. Raddle's anger rose through an indignant *crescendo*, on Ben Allen's remonstrating, "But you are such an unreasonable woman"—to the sharp and biting interrogation, "I beg your parding, young man, but will you have the goodness to call me that again, sir?"

BEN ALLEN, meekly and somewhat uneasy on his own account,—"I didn't make use of the word in any invidious sense, ma'am."

LANDLADY, louder and more imperatively,—"I beg your parding, young man, but *who* do you call a woman? Did you make that remark to *me*, sir?"

"*Why, bless my heart!*"

"Did you apply that name to me, I ask of you, sir?"

On his answering, Well, of course he did!—then, as she retreated towards the open room-door, came the last outburst of her invectives, high-pitched in their voluble utterance, against him, against them both, against everybody, including Mr. Raddle in the kitchen —"a base, faint-hearted, timorous wretch, that's afraid to come upstairs and face the ruffinly creaturs—that's *afraid* to come—that's AFRAID!" Ending with her screaming descent of the stairs in the midst of a loud double-knock, upon the arrival just then of the Pickwickians, when, "in an uncontrollable burst of mental agony," Mrs. Raddle threw down all the umbrellas in the passage, disappearing into the back parlour with an awful crash. In answer to the cheerful inquiry from Mr. Pickwick,—"Does Mr. Sawyer live here?" came the lugubrious and monotonously intoned response, all on one note, of the aboriginal young person, the gal Betsey (one of the minor characters in the original chapter, and yet, as already remarked, a superlatively good impersonation in the Reading)—"Yes; first-floor. It's the door straight afore you when you get's to the top of the stairs"—with which the dirty slipshod in black cotton stockings disappeared with the candle down the kitchen stair-case, leaving the unfortunate arrivals to grope their way up as they best could. Welcomed rather dejectedly by Bob on the first-floor landing, where Mr. Pickwick put, not, as in the original work, his hat, but, in the Reading, "his foot" in the tray of glasses, they were very soon followed, one after another, by the remainder of the visitors. Notably by a sentimental young gentleman with a nice sense of honour, and, most notably of all (with a heavy footstep, very welcome indeed whenever heard) by Jack Hopkins. Jack was at once the Hamlet and the Yorick of the whole entertainment—all-essential to it—whose very look (with his chin rather stiff in the stock), whose very words (short, sharp, and decisive) had about them a drily and all-but indescribably humorous effect.

As spoken by the Novelist himself, Jack Hopkins's every syllable told to perfection. His opening report immediately on his arrival, of "rather a good accident" just brought into the casualty ward—only, it was true, a man fallen out of a four-pair-of-stairs window; but a very fair case, *very* fair case indeed!—was of itself a dexterous forefinger between the small ribs to begin with. Would the patient recover? Well, no—with an air of supreme indifference—no, he should rather say he wouldn't. But there must be a splendid operation, though, on the morrow—magnificent sight if Slasher did it! Did he consider Mr. Slasher a good operator? "Best alive: took a boy's leg out of the socket last week—boy ate five apples and a gingerbread cake exactly two minutes after it was all over;—boy said he wouldn't lie there to be made game of; and he'd tell his mother if they didn't begin." To hear Dickens say this in the short, sharp utterances of Jack Hopkins, to see his manner in recounting it, stiff-necked, and with a glance under the drooping eyelids in the direction of Mr. Pickwick's listening face, was only the next best thing to hearing him and seeing him, still in the person of Jack Hopkins, relate the memorable anecdote about the child swallowing the necklace—pronounced in Jack Hopkins's abbreviated articulation of it, *neck-luss*—a word repeated by him a round dozen times at the least within a few seconds in the reading version of that same anecdote. How characteristically and comically the abbreviations were multiplied for the delivery of it, by the very voice and in the very person, as it were, of Jack Hopkins, who shall say! As, for example—"Sister, industrious girl, seldom treated herself to bit of finery, cried eyes out, at loss of—neck-luss; looked high and low for—neck-luss. Few days afterwards, family at dinner—baked shoulder of mutton and potatoes, child wasn't hungry, playing about the room, when family suddenly heard devil of a noise like small hail-storm." How abbreviated passages like these look, as compared with the original—could only be rendered comprehensible upon the instant, by giving in this place a facsimile of one of the pages relating to Jack Hopkins's immortal story about the—neck-luss, exactly as it appears in the marked copy of the Reading of "Mr. Bob Sawyer's Party," a page covered all over, as will be observed, with minute touches in the Novelist's own handwriting.

Nothing at all in the later version of this Reading was said about the prim person in cloth boots, who unsuccessfully attempted all through the evening to make a joke. Of him the readers of "Pickwick" will very well remember it to have been related that he commenced a long story about a great public character, whose name he had forgotten, making a particularly happy reply to another illustrious individual whom he had never been able to identify, and, after enlarging with great minuteness upon divers collateral circumstances distantly connected with the anecdote, could not for the life of him recollect at that precise moment what the anecdote was—although he had been in the habit, for the last ten years, of telling the story with great applause! While disposed to regret the omission of this preposterously natural incident from the revised version of the Reading, and especially Bob Sawyer's concluding remark in regard to it, that he should very much like to hear the end of it, for, *so far as it went,* it was, without exception, the very best story he had ever heard"—we were more than compensated by another revisive touch, by which Mr. Hopkins, instead of Mr. Gunter, in the pink shirt, was represented as one of the two interlocutors in the famous quarrel-scene: the other being Mr. Noddy, the scorbutic youth, with the nice sense of honour. Through this modification the ludicrous effect of the squabble was wonderfully enhanced, as where Mr. Noddy, having been threatened with being "pitched out o' window" by Mr. Jack Hopkins, said to the latter, "I should like to see you do it, sir," Jack Hopkins curtly retaliating—"You shall *feel* me do it, sir, in half a minute." The reconciliation of the two attained its climax of absurdity in the Reading, when Mr. Noddy, having gradually allowed his feelings to overpower him, professed that he had ever entertained a devoted personal attachment to Mr. Hopkins. Consequent upon this, Mr. Hopkins, we were told, replied, that, "on the whole, he rather preferred Mr. Noddy to his own *mother*"—the word standing, of course, as "brother" in the original. Summing it all up, the Reader would then add, with a rise and fall of the voice at almost every other word in the sentence, the mere sound of which was inexpressibly ludicrous—"Everybody said the whole dispute had been conducted in a manner" (here he would sometimes gag) "that did equal credit to the head and heart of both parties concerned."

Another gag, of which there is no sign in the marked copy, those who attended any later delivery of this Reading will well remember he was fond of introducing. This was immediately after Mrs. Raddle had put an end to the evening's enjoyment in the very middle of Jack Hopkins' song (with a chorus) of "The King, God bless him," carolled forth by Jack to a novel air compounded of the "Bay of Biscay" and "A Frog he would a-wooing go"—when poor, discomfited Bob (after turning pale at the voice of his dreaded landlady, shrilly calling out, "Mr. Saw-*yer!* Mr. Saw-*yer!*") turned reproachfully on the over-boisterous Jack Hopkins, with, "I *thought* you were making too much noise, Jack. You're such a fellow for chorusing! You're always at it. You came into the world chorusing; and I believe you'll go out of it chorusing." Through their appreciation of which—more even than through their remembrance of Mrs. Raddle's withdrawal of her nightcap, with a scream, from over the staircase banisters, on catching sight of Mr. Pickwick, saying, "Get along with you, you old wretch! Old enough to be his grandfather, you willin! You're worse than any of 'em!"—the hearers paid to the Reader of Bob Sawyer's Party their last tribute of laughter.

THE CHIMES.

As poetical in its conception, and also, intermittently, in its treatment, as anything he ever wrote, this Goblin Story of Some Bells that Rang an Old Year Out and a New Year In, was, in those purely goblin, or more intensely imaginative portions of it,one of the most effective of our Author's Readings. Hence its selection by him for his very first Reading on his own account in St. Martin's Hall, Long Acre. Listening, as we did, then and afterwards, to the tale, as it was told by his own sympathetic lips, much of the incongruity, otherwise no doubt apparent in the narrative, seemed at those times to disappear altogether. The incongruity, we mean, observable between the queer little ticket-porter and the elfin phantoms of the belfry; between Trotty Veck, in his "breezy, goose-skinned, blue-nosed, red-eyed, stony-toed, tooth-chattering" stand-point by the old church-door, and the Goblin Sight beheld by him when he had clambered up, up, up among the roof-beams of the great church-tower. As the story was related in its original form, it was rung out befittingly from the Chimes in four quarters. As a Reading it was subdivided simply into three parts.

Nothing whatever was preserved (by an error as it always seemed to us) of the admirable introduction. The story-teller piqued no one into attention by saying—to begin with—"There are not many people who would care to sleep in a church." Adding immediately, with delightful particularity, "I don't mean at sermon time in warm weather (when the thing has actually been done once or twice), but in the night, and alone." Not a word was uttered in the exordium of the Reading about the dismal trick the night-wind has in those ghostly hours of wandering round and round a building of that sort, and moaning as it goes; of its trying with a secret hand the windows and the doors, fumbling for some crevice by which to enter, and, having got in, "as one not finding what it seeks, whatever that may be," of its wailing and howling to issue forth again; of its stalking through the aisles and gliding round and round the pillars, and "tempting the deep organ;" of its soaring up to the roof, and after striving vainly to rend the rafters, flinging itself despairingly upon the stones below, and passing mutteringly into the vaults! Anon, coming up stealthily—the Christmas book goes on to say—"It has a ghostly sound, lingering within the Altar, where it seems to chant in its wild way of Wrong and Murder done, and false Gods worshipped, in defiance of the Tables of the Law, which look so fair and smooth, but are so flawed and broken. Ugh!

Heaven preserve us, sitting snugly round the fire!—it has an awful voice that Wind at Midnight, singing in a church!" Of all this and of yet more to the like purpose, not one syllable was there in the Reading, which, on the contrary, began at once point-blank: "High up in the steeple of an old church, far above the town, and far below the clouds, dwelt the 'Chimes' I tell of." Directly after which the Reader, having casually mentioned the circumstance of their just then striking twelve at noon, gave utterance to Trotty Veck's ejaculatory reflection: "Dinner-time, eh? Ah! There's nothing more regular in its coming round than dinner-time, and there's nothing less regular in its coming round than dinner." Followed by his innocently complacent exclamation: "I wonder whether it would be worth any gentleman's while, now, to buy that obserwation for the Papers, or the Parliament!" The Reader adding upon the instant, with an explanatory aside, that "Trotty was only joking," striving to console himself doubtless for the exceeding probability there was before him, at the moment, of his going, not for the first time, dinnerless.

In the thick of his meditations Trotty was startled —those who ever attended this Reading will remember how pleasantly—by the unlooked-for appearance of his pretty daughter Meg. "And not alone!" as she told him cheerily. "Why you don't mean to say," was the wondering reply of the old ticket-porter, looking curiously the while at a covered basket carried in Margaret's hand, "that you have brought——" Hadn't she! It was burning hot—scalding! He must guess from the steaming flavour what it was! Thereupon came the by-play of the Humorist—after the fashion of Munden, who, according to Charles Lamb, "understood a leg of mutton in its quiddity." It was thus with the Reader when he syllabled, with watering lips, guess after guess at the half-opened basket. "It ain't—I suppose it ain't polonies? [sniffing]. No. It's—it's mellower than polonies. It's too decided for trotters. Liver? No. There's a mildness about it that don't answer to liver. Pettitoes? No. It ain't faint enough for pettitoes. It wants the stringiness of cock's heads. And I know it ain't sausages. I'll tell you what it is. No, it isn't, neither. Why, what am I thinking of! I shall forget my own name next. It's tripe!" Forthwith, to reward him for having thus hit it off at last so cleverly, Meg, as she expressed it, with a flourish, laid the cloth, meaning the pocket-handkerchief in which the basin of tripe had been tied up, and actually offered the sybarite who was going to enjoy the unexpected banquet, a choice of dining-places! "Where will you dine, father? On the post, or on the steps? How grand we are: two places to choose from!" The weather being dry, and the steps therefore chosen, those being rheumatic only in the damp, Trotty Veck was not merely represented by the Reader as feasting upon the tripe, but as listening meanwhile to Meg's account of how it had all been arranged that she and her lover Richard should, upon the very next day, that is, upon New Year's Day, be married.

In the midst of this agreeable confabulation—Richard himself having in the interim become one of the party—the little old ticket-porter, the pretty daughter, and the sturdy young blacksmith, were suddenly scattered. The Reader went on to relate how this happened, with ludicrous accuracy, upon the abrupt opening of the door, around the steps of which they were gathered—a flunkey nearly putting his foot in the tripe, with this indignant apostrophe, "Out of the vays, here, will you? You must always go and be a settin' on our steps, must you? You can't go and give a turn to none of the neighbours never, can't you?" Adding, even, a moment afterwards, with an aggrieved air of almost affecting expostulation, "You're always a being begged and prayed upon your bended knees, you are, to let our door-steps be? CAN'T you let 'em be?" Nothing more was seen or heard of that footman, and yet in the utterance of those few words of his the individuality of the man somehow was thoroughly realised. Observing him, listening to him, as he stood there palpably before us, one seemed to understand better than ever Thackeray's declaration in regard to those same menials in plush breeches, that a certain delightful "quivering swagger" of the calves about them, had for him always, as he expressed it, "a frantic fascination!" Immediately afterwards, however, as the Reader turned a new leaf, in place of the momentary apparition of that particular flunkey, three very different persons appeared to step across the threshold on to the platform. Low-spirited, Mr. Filer, with his hands in his trousers-pockets. The red-faced gentleman who was always vaunting, under the title of the "good old times," some undiscoverable past which he perpetually lamented as his deceased Millennium. And finally—as large as life, and as real—Alderman Cute. As in the original Christmas book, so also in the Reading, the one flagrant improbability was the consumption by Alderman Cute of the last lukewarm tid-bit of tripe left by Trotty Veck down at the bottom of the basin—its consumption, indeed, by any alderman, however prying or gluttonous. Barring that, the whole of the first scene of the "Chimes" was alive with reality, and with a curious diversity of human character. In the one that followed, and in which Trotty conveyed a letter to Sir Joseph Bowley, the impersonation of the obese hall-porter, later on identified as Tugby, was in every way far beyond that of the pompous humanitarian member of parliament. A hall-porter this proved to be whose voice, when he had found it—"which it took him some time to do, for it was a long way off, and hidden under a load of meat"—was, in truth, as the Author's lips expressed it, and as his pen had long before described it in the book, "a fat whisper." Afterwards when re-introduced, Tugby hardly, as it appeared to us, came up to the original description. When the stout old lady, his supposititious wife, formerly, or rather really, all through, Mrs. Chickenstalker, says, in answer to his inquiries as to the weather, one especially bitter winter's evening, "Blowing and sleeting hard, and threatening snow. Dark, and very cold"—Tugby's almost apoplectic reply was delicious, no doubt, in its suffocative delivery. "I'm glad to think we had muffins for tea, my dear. It's a sort of night that's meant for muffins. Likewise crumpets; also Sally Lunns." But, for all that, we invariably missed the sequel—which, once missed, could hardly be foregone contentedly. We recalled to mind, for example, such descriptive particulars in the original story as that, in mentioning each successive kind of eatable, Tugby did so "as if he were musingly summing up his good actions," or that, after this, rubbing his fat legs and jerking them at the knees to get the fire upon the yet unroasted parts, he laughed as if somebody had tickled him! We bore distinctly enough in remembrance, and longed then to have heard from the lips of the Reader—in answer to the dream-wife's remark, "You're in spirits, Tugby, my dear!"—Tugby's fat, gasping response, "No,—No. Not particular. I'm a little elewated. The muffins came so pat!" Though, even if that addition had been vouchsafed, we should still, no doubt, have hungered for the descriptive particulars that followed, relating not only how the former hall-porter chuckled until he was black in the face—having so much ado, in fact, to become any other colour, that his fat legs made the strangest excursions into the air—but that Mrs. Tugby, that is, Chickenstalker, after thumping him violently on the back, and shaking him as if he were a bottle, was constrained to cry out, in great terror, "Good gracious, goodness, lord-a-mercy, bless and save the man! What's he a-doing?" To which all that Mr. Tugby can faintly reply, as he wipes his eyes, is, that he finds himself a little "elewated!"

Another omission in the Reading was, if possible, yet more surprising, namely, the whole of Will Fern's finest speech: an address full of rustic eloquence that one can't help feeling sure would have told wonderfully as Dickens could have delivered it. However, the story, foreshortened though it was, precisely as he related it, was told with a due regard to its artistic completeness. Margaret and Lilian, the old ticket-porter and the young blacksmith, were the principal interlocutors. Like the melodrama of Victorine, it all turned out, of course, to be no more than "the baseless fabric of a vision," the central incidents of the tale, at any rate, being composed of "such stuff as dreams are made of." How it all came to be evolved by the "Chimes" from the slumbering brain of the queer, little old ticket-porter was related more fully and more picturesquely, no doubt, in the printed narrative, but in the Reading, at the least, it was depicted with more dramatic force and passion. The merest glimmering, however, was afforded of the ghostly or elfin spectacle, as seen by the "mind's eye" of the dreamer, and which in the book itself was so important an integral portion of the tale, as there unfolded, constituting, as it did, for that matter, the very soul or spirit of what was meant by "The Chimes."

Speaking of the collective chimes of a great city, Victor Hugo has remarked in his prose masterpiece that, in an ordinary way, the noise issuing from a vast capital is the talking of the city, that at night it is the breathing of the city, but that when the bells are ringing it is the singing of the city. Descanting upon this congenial theme, the poet-novelist observes, in continuation, that while at first the vibrations of each bell rise straight, pure, and in a manner separate from that of the others, swelling by degrees, they blend, melt, and amalgamate in magnificent concert until they become at length one mass of sonorous vibrations, which, issuing incessantly from innumerable steeples, float, undulate, bound, whirl over the city, expanding at last far beyond the horizon the deafening circle of their oscillations. What has been said thus superbly, though it may be somewhat extravagantly, by Hugo, in regard to "that *tutti* of steeples, that column of sound, that cloud or sea of harmony," as he variously terms it, has been said less extravagantly, but quite as exquisitely, by

Charles Dickens, in regard to the chimes of a single belfry. After this New Year's tale of his was first told, there rang out from the opposite shores of the Atlantic, that most wonderful tintinnabulation in all literature, "The Bells" of Edgar Poe—which is, among minor poems, in regard to the belfry, what Southey's "Lodore" is to the cataract, full, sonorous, and exhaustive. And there it is, in that marvellous little poem of "The Bells," that the American lyrist, as it has always seemed to us, has caught much of the eltrich force and beauty and poetic significance of "The Chimes" as they were originally rung forth in the prose-poetry of the English novelist:—

"And the people—ah, the people—
They that dwell up in the steeple,
All alone,
And who tolling, tolling, tolling,
In that muffled monotone,
Feel a glory in so rolling
On [or from] the human heart a stone—
They are neither man nor woman—
They are neither brute nor human—
They are Ghouls:
And their king it is who tolls;
And he rolls, rolls, rolls,
Rolls
A pæan from the bells."

Charles Dickens, in his beautiful imaginings in regard to the Spirits of the Bells—something of the grace and goblinry of which, Maclise's pencil shadowed forth in the lovely frontispiece to the little volume in the form in which it was first of all published—has exhausted the vocabulary of wonder in his elvish delineation of the Goblin Sight beheld in the old church-tower on New Year's Eve by the awe-stricken ticket-porter.

In the Reading one would naturally have liked to have caught some glimpse at least of the swarming out to view of the "dwarf-phantoms, spirits, elfin creatures of the Bells;" to have seen them "leaping, flying, dropping, pouring from the Bells," unceasingly; to have realised them anew as a listener, just as the imaginary dreamer beheld them all about him in his vision—"round him on the ground, above him in the air, clambering from him by the ropes below, looking down upon him from the massive iron-girded beams, peeping in upon him through the chinks and loopholes in the walls, spreading away and away from him in enlarging circles, as the water-ripples give place to a huge stone that suddenly comes plashing in among them." In their coming and in their going, the sight, it will be remembered, was equally marvellous. Whether—as the Chimes rang out—we read of the dream-haunted, "He saw them [these swarming goblins] ugly, handsome, crippled, exquisitely formed. He saw them young, he saw them old, he saw them kind, he saw them cruel, he saw them merry, he saw them grim, he saw them dance, he heard them sing, he saw them tear their hair, and heard them howl"—diving, soaring, sailing, perching, violently active in their restlessness—stone, brick, slate, tile, transparent to the dreamer's gaze, and pervious to their movements—the bells all the while in an uproar, the great church tower vibrating from parapet to basement! Or, whether—when the Chimes ceased—there came that instantaneous transformation! "The whole swarm fainted; their forms collapsed, their speed deserted them; they sought to fly, but in the act of falling died and melted into air. One straggler," says the book, "leaped down pretty briskly from the surface of the Great Bell, and alighted on his feet, but he was dead and gone before he could turn round." After it has been added that some thus gambolling in the tower "remained there, spinning over and over a little longer," becoming fainter, fewer, feebler, and so vanishing—we read, "The last of all was one small hunchback, who had got into an echoing corner, where he twirled and twirled, and floated by himself a long time; showing such perseverance, that at last he dwindled to a leg, and even to a foot, before he finally retired; but he vanished in the end, and then the tower was silent." Nothing of this, however, was given in the Reading, the interest of which was almost entirely restricted to the fancied fluctuation of fortunes among the human characters. All of the pathetic and most of the comic portions of the tale were happily preserved. When, in the persons of the Tugbys, "fat company, rosy-cheeked company, comfortable company," came to be introduced, there was an instant sense of exhilaration among the audience.

A roar invariably greeted the remark, "They were but two, but they were red enough for ten." Similarly pronounced was the reception of the casual announcement of the "stone pitcher of terrific size," in which the good wife brought her contribution of "a little flip" to the final merry-making. "Mrs. Chickenstalker's notion of a little flip did honour to her character," elicited a burst of laughter that was instantly renewed when the Reader added, that "the pitcher reeked like a volcano," and that "the man who carried it was faint." The Drum, by the way—braced tight enough, as any one might admit in the original narrative—seemed rather slackened, and was certainly less effective, in the Reading. One listened in vain for the well-remembered parenthesis indicative of its being the man himself, and not the instrument. "The Drum (who was a private friend of Trotty's) then stepped forward, and" offered—evidently with a hiccough or two—his greeting of good fellowship, "which," as we learn from the book, "was received with a general shout." The Humorist added thereupon, in his character as Storyteller, not in his capacity as Reader, "The Drum was rather drunk, by-the-bye; but never mind." A band of music, with marrow-bones and cleavers and a set of hand-bells—clearly all of them under the direction of the Drum—then struck up the dance at Meg's wedding. But, after due mention had been made of how Trotty danced with Mrs. Chickenstalker "in a step unknown before or since, founded on his own peculiar trot," the story closed in the book, and closed also in the Reading, with words that, in their gentle and harmonious flow, seemed to come from the neighbouring church-tower as final echoes from "The Chimes" themselves.

THE STORY OF LITTLE DOMBEY.

THE hushed silence with which the concluding passages of this Reading were always listened to, spoke more eloquently than any applause could possibly have done, of the sincerity of the emotions it awakened. A cursory glance at the audience confirmed the impression produced by that earlier evidence of their rapt and breathless attention. It is the simplest truth to say that at those times many a face illustrated involuntarily the loveliest line in the noblest ode in the language, where Dryden has sung even of a warrior—

> "And now and then a sigh he heaved,
> And tears began to flow."

The subdued voice of the Reader, moreover, accorded tenderly with one's remembrance of his own acknowledgment ten years after his completion of the book from which this story was extracted, that with a heavy heart he had walked the streets of Paris alone during the whole of one winter's night, while he and his little friend parted company for ever! Charles Young's

"I mean, Papa, what can it do?"

Mr Dombey ~~drew his chair back to its former place and patted him on the head~~. "You'll know better bye-and-bye, my man Money, Paul, can do anything."

[It isn't cruel; is it?" "No, a good thing can't be cruel

and isn't cruel

"If money can do anything, I wonder it didn't save me my Mama. It can't make me strong and quite well, either. I am so tired sometimes and my bones ache so, that I don't know what to do!"

As you are so rich.

son, the vicar of Ilminster, has, recently, in his own Diary appended to his memoir of his father, the tragedian, related a curious anecdote, illustrative, in a very striking way, of the grief—the profound and overwhelming grief—excited in a mind and heart like those of Lord Jeffrey, by the imaginary death of another of these dream-children of Charles Dickens. The editor of the *Edinburgh Review*, we there read, was surprised by Mrs. Henry Siddons, seated in his library, with his head on the table, crying. "Delicately retiring," we are then told, "in the hope that her entrance had been unnoticed," Mrs. Siddons observed that Jeffrey raised his head and was kindly beckoning her back. The Diary goes on: "Perceiving that his cheek was flushed and his eyes suffused with tears, she apologised for her intrusion, and begged permission to withdraw. When he found that she was seriously intending to leave him, he rose from his chair, took her by both hands, and led her to a seat." Then came the acknowledgment prefaced by Lord Jeffrey's remark that he was "a great goose to have given way so." Little Nell was dead! The newly published number of "Master Humphrey's Clock" (No. 44) was lying before him, in which he had just been reading of the general bereavement!

Referring to another of these little creatures' deaths, that of Tiny Tim, Thackeray wrote in the July number of *Fraser*, for 1844, that there was one passage regarding it about which a man would hardly venture to speak in print or in public " any more than he would of any other affections of his private heart."

It has been related, even of the burly demagogue, O'Connell, that on first reading of Nell's death in the Old Curiosity Shop, he exclaimed—his eyes running over with tears while he flung the leaves indignantly out of the window—" he should not have killed her—he should not have killed her: she was too good!"

Finally, another Scotch critic and judge, Lord Cockburn, writing to the Novelist on the very morrow of reading the memorable fifth number of " Dombey and Son," in which the death of Little Paul is so exquisitely depicted—offering his grateful acknowledgments to the Author for the poignant grief he had caused him—added, " I have felt my heart purified by those tears, and blessed and loved you for making me shed them."

Hardly can it be matter for wonder, therefore, remarking how the printed pages would draw such tokens of sympathy from men like Cockburn, and Jeffrey, and Thackeray, and O'Connell, that a mixed audience showed traces of emotion when the profoundly sympathetic voice of Dickens himself related this story of the Life and Death of Little Dombey. Yet the pathetic beauty of the tale, for all that, was only dimly hinted at throughout,—the real pathos of it, indeed, being only fully indicated almost immediately before its conclusion. Earlier in the Reading, in fact, the drollery of the comic characters introduced—of themselves irresistible—would have been simply paramount, but for the incidental mention of the mother's death, when clinging to that frail spar within her arms, her little daughter, "she drifted out upon the dark and unknown sea that rolls round all the world." Paul's little wistful face looked out every now and then, it is true, from among the fantastic forms and features grouped around him, with a growing sense upon the hearer of what was really meant by the child being so "old-fashioned." But the ludicrous effect of those surrounding characters was nothing less than all-mastering in its predominance.

There was Mrs. Pipchin, for example, that grim old lady with a mottled face like bad marble, who acquired an immense reputation as a manager of children, by the simple device of giving them everything they didn't like and nothing that they did! Whose constitution required mutton chops hot and hot, and buttered toast in similar relays! And with whom one of Little Dombey's earliest dialogues in the Reading awakened invariably such bursts of hearty laughter! Seated in his tall, spindle-legged arm-chair by the fire, staring steadily at the exemplary Pipchin, Little Paul, we were told, was asked [in the most snappish voice possible], by that austere female, What he was thinking about?

"You," [in the gentlest childlike voice] said Paul, without the least reserve.

"And what are you thinking about me?"

"I'm—thinking—how old—you must be."

"You mustn't say such things as that, young gentleman. That'll never do."

"Why not [slowly and wonderingly]?"

"Never you mind, sir [shorter and sharper than ever]. Remember the story of the little boy that was gored to death by a mad bull for asking questions."

"If the bull [in a high falsetto voice and with greater deliberation than ever] was mad, how did he know that the boy asked questions? Nobody can go and whisper secrets to a mad bull. I don't believe that story."

Little Dombey's fellow-sufferers at Mrs. Pipchin's were hardly less ludicrous in their way than that bitter old victim of the Peruvian mines in her perennial weeds of black bombazeen. Miss Pankey, for instance, the mild little blue-eyed morsel of a child who was instructed by the Ogress that "nobody who sniffed before visitors ever went to heaven!" And her associate in misery, one Master Bitherstone, from India, who objected so much to the Pipchinian system, that before Little Dombey had been in the house five minutes, he privately consulted that gentleman if he could afford him any idea of the way back to Bengal! What the Pipchinian system was precisely, the Reader indicated perhaps the most happily by his way of saying, that instead of its encouraging a child's mind to develop itself, like a flower, it strove to open it by force, like an oyster. Fading slowly away while he is yet under Mrs. Pipchin's management, poor little

Paul, as the audience well knew, was removed on to Doctor Blimber's Academy for Young Gentlemen. There the humorous company gathered around Paul immediately increased. But, before his going amongst them, the Reader enabled us more vividly to realise, by an additional touch or two, the significance of the peculiarity of being "old fashioned," for which the fading child appeared in everybody's eyes so remarkable.

Wheeled down to the beach in a little invalid-carriage, he would cling fondly to his sister Florence. He would say to any chance child who might come to bear him company [in a soft, drawling, half-querulous voice, and with the gravest look], "Go away, if you please. Thank you, but I don't want you." He would wonder to himself and to Floy what the waves were always saying—always saying! At about the middle of the 47th page of the Reading copy of this book about Little Dombey, the copy from which Dickens Read, both in England and America, there is, in his handwriting, the word—"Pause." It occurs just in between Little Dombey's confiding to his sister, that if she were in India he should die of being so sorry and so lonely! and the incident of his suddenly waking up at another time from a long sleep in his little carriage on the shingles, to ask her, not only What the rolling waves are saying so constantly, but What place is over there?—far away!—looking eagerly, as he inquires, towards some invisible region beyond the horizon! That momentary pause will be very well remembered by everyone who attended this Reading.

One single omission we are still disposed to regret in the putting together of the materials for this particular Reading from the original narrative. In approaching Dr. Blimber's establishment for the first time, we would gladly have witnessed the sparring-match, as one may say, on the very threshold, between Mrs. Pipchin the Ogress in bombazeen and the weak-eyed young man-servant who opens the door! The latter of whom, having "the first faint streaks or early dawn of a grin on his countenance—(it was mere imbecility)" as the Author himself explains parenthetically—Mrs. Pipchin at once takes it into her head, is inspired by impudence, and snaps at accordingly. Of this we saw nothing, however, in the Reading. We heard nothing of Mrs. Pipchin's explosive, "How dare you laugh behind the gentleman's back?" or of the weak-eyed young man's answering in consternation, "I ain't a laughing at nobody, ma'am." Any more than of the Ogress saying a while later, "You're laughing again, sir!" or of the young man, grievously oppressed, repudiating the charge with, "I *ain't*. I never see such a thing as this!" The old lady as she passed on with, "Oh! he was a precious fellow," leaving him, who was in fact all meekness and incapacity, "affected even to tears by the incident." If we saw nothing, however, of that retainer of Dr. Blimber, we were introduced to another, meaning the blue-coated, bright-buttoned butler, "who gave quite a winey flavour to the table-beer—he poured it out so superbly!" We had Dr. Blimber himself, besides, with his learned legs, like a clerical pianoforte—a bald head, highly polished, and a chin so double, it was a wonder how he ever managed to shave into the creases. We had Miss Blimber, in spectacles, like a ghoul, "dry and sandy with working in the graves of deceased languages." We had Mrs. Blimber, not learned herself, but pretending to be so, which did quite as well, languidly exclaiming at evening parties, that if she could have known Cicero, she thought she could have died contented. We had Mr. Feeder, clipped to the stubble, grinding out his classic stops like a barrel-organ of erudition. Above all, we had Toots, the head boy, or rather "the head and shoulder boy," he was so much taller than the rest! Of whom in that intellectual forcing-house (where he had "gone through" everything so completely, that one day he "suddenly left off blowing, and remained in the establishment a mere stalk") people had come at last to say, "that the Doctor had rather overdone it with young Toots, and that when he began to have whiskers he left off having brains." From the moment when Young Toots's voice was first heard, in tones so deep, and in a manner so sheepish, that "if a lamb had roared it couldn't have been more surprising," saying to Little Dombey with startling suddenness, "How are you?"—every time the Reader opened his lips, as speaking in that character, there was a burst of merriment. His boastful account always called forth laughter—that his tailor was Burgess and Co., "fash'nable, but very dear." As also did his constantly reiterated inquiries of Paul—always as an entirely new idea—"I say—it's not of the slightest consequence, you know, but I should wish to mention it—how are you, you know?" Hardly less provocative of mirth was Briggs's confiding one evening to Little Dombey, that his head ached ready to split, and "that he should wish himself dead if it wasn't for his mother and a blackbird he had at home."

Wonderful fun used to be made by the Reader of the various incidents at the entertainment given upon the eve of the vacations by Doctor and Mrs. Blimber to the Young Gentlemen and their Friends, when "the hour was half-past seven o'clock, and the object was quadrilles." The Doctor pacing up and down in the drawing-room, full dressed, before anybody had arrived, "with a dignified and unconcerned demeanour, as if he thought it barely possible that one or two people might drop in by-and-by!" His exclaiming, when Mr. Toots and Mr. Feeder were announced by the butler, and as if he were extremely surprised to see them, "Aye, aye, aye! God bless my soul!" Mr. Toots, one blaze of jewellery and buttons, so undecided, "on a calm revision of all the circumstances," whether it were better to have his waistcoat fastened or unfastened both at top and bottom, as the arrivals thickened, so influencing him by the force of example, that at the last he was "continually fingering that article of dress as if he were performing on some instrument!" Thoroughly enjoyable though the whole scene was in its throng of ludicrous particulars, it merely led the way up appreciably and none the less tenderly, for all the innocent laughter, to the last and supremely pathetic incidents of the story as related thenceforth (save only for one startling instant) *sotto voce*, by the Reader.

The exceptional moment here alluded to, when his voice was suddenly raised, to be hushed again the instant afterwards, came at the very opening of the final scene by Little Dombey's death-bed, where the sunbeams, towards evening, struck through the rustling blinds and quivered on the opposite wall like golden water. Overwhelmed, as little Paul was occasionally, with "his only trouble," a sense of the swift and rapid river, "he felt forced," the Reader went on to say, "to try and stop it—to stem it with his childish hands, or choke its way with sand—and when he saw it coming on, resistless, HE CRIED OUT!" Dropping his voice from that abrupt outcry instantly afterwards, to the gentlest tones, as he added, "But a word from Florence, who was always at his side, restored him to himself"—the Reader continued in those subdued and tender accents to the end.

The child's pity for his father's sorrowing, was surpassed only, as all who witnessed this Reading will readily recollect, by the yet more affecting scene with his old nurse. Waking upon a sudden, on the last of the many evenings, when the golden water danced in shining ripples on the wall, waking mind and body, sitting upright in his bed—

"And who is this? *Is* this my old nurse?" asked the child, regarding with a radiant smile a figure coming in.

"Yes, yes. No other stranger would have shed those tears at sight of him, and called him her dear boy, her pretty boy, her own poor blighted child. No other woman would have stooped down by his bed and taken up his wasted hand and put it to her lips and breast, as one who had some right to fondle it. No other woman would have so forgotten everybody there but him and Floy, and been so full of tenderness and pity."

The child's words coming then so lovingly: "Floy! this is a kind good face! I am glad to see it again. Don't go away, old nurse! Stay here! *Good bye!*" prepared one exquisitely for the rest. "Not good-bye?" "Ah, yes! good-bye!"

Then the end! The child having been laid down again with his arms clasped round his sister's neck, telling her that the stream was lulling him to rest, that now the boat was out at sea and that there was shore before him, and—Who stood upon the bank! Putting his hands together "as he had been used to do at his prayers"—not removing his arms to do it, but folding them so behind his sister's neck—"Mamma is like you, Floy!" he cried; "I know her by the face! But tell them that the picture on the stairs at school is not Divine enough. The light about the head is shining on me as I go!"

Then came two noble passages, nobly delivered.

First—when there were no eyes unmoistened among the listeners—

"The golden ripple on the wall came back again, and nothing else stirred in the room. The old, old fashion! The fashion that came in with our first garments, and will last unchanged until our race has run its course, and the wide firmament is rolled up like a scroll. The old, old fashion—Death!"

And lastly—with a tearful voice—

"Oh, thank God, all who see it, for that older fashion yet of Immortality! And look upon us, Angels of young children, with regards not quite estranged, when the swift river bears us to the ocean!"

Remembering which exquisite words as he himself delivered them, having the very tones of his voice still ringing tenderly in our recollection, the truth of that beautiful remark of Dean Stanley's comes back anew as though it were now only for the first time realised, where, in his funeral sermon of the 19th June, 1870, he said that it was the inculcation of the lesson derived from precisely such a scene as this which will always make the grave of Charles Dickens seem "as though it were the very grave of those little innocents whom he created for our companionship, for our instruction, for our delight and solace." The little workhouse-boy, the little orphan girl, the little cripple, who "not only blessed his father's needy home, but softened the rude stranger's hardened conscience," were severally referred to by the preacher when he gave this charming thought its affecting application. But, foremost among these bewitching children of the Novelist's imagination, might surely be placed the child-hero of a story closing hardly so much with his death as with his apotheosis.

MR. CHOPS, THE DWARF.

It remains still a matter of surprise how so much was made out of this slight sketch by the simple force of its humorous delivery. "Mr. Chops, the Dwarf," as, indeed, was only befitting, was the smallest of all the Readings. The simple little air that so caught the dreamer's fancy, when played upon the harp by Scrooge's niece by marriage, is described after all, as may be remembered by the readers of the Carol, to to have been intrinsically "a mere nothing; you might learn to whistle it in two minutes." Say that in twenty minutes, or, at the outside, in half-an-hour, any ordinarily glib talker might have rattled through these comic recollections of Mr. Magsman, yet, when rattled through by Dickens, the laughter awakened seems now in the retrospect to have been altogether out of proportion. In itself the subject was anything but attractive, relating, as it did, merely to the escapade of a monstrosity. The surroundings are ignoble, the language is illiterate, the narrative from first to last is characterised by its grotesque extravagance. Yet the whole is presented to view in so utterly ludicrous an aspect, that one needs must laugh just as surely as one listened. Turning over the leaves now, and recalling to mind the hilarity they used to excite even among the least impressionable audience whenever they were fluttered (there are not a dozen of them altogether) on the familiar reading-desk, one marvels over the success of such an exceedingly small oddity as over the remembrance, let us say, of the brilliant performance of a fantasia on the jew's-harp by Eulenstein.

Nevertheless, slight though it is, the limning all through has touches of the most comic suggestiveness. Magsman's account of the show-house during his occupancy is sufficiently absurd to begin with—"the picter of the giant who was himself the heighth of the house," being run up with a line and pulley to a pole on the roof till "his 'ed was coeval with the parapet;" the picter of the child of the British Planter seized by two Boa Constrictors, "not that *we* never had no child, nor no Constrictors either;" similarly, the picter of the Wild Ass of the Prairies, "not that *we* never had no wild asses, nor wouldn't have had 'em at a gift." And to crown all, the picter of the Dwarf—who was "a uncommon small man, he really was. Certainly not so small as he was made out to be; but where *is* your Dwarf as is?" A picter "like him, too (considerin'), with George the Fourth, in such a state of astonishment at him as his Majesty couldn't with his utmost politeness and stoutness express." Wrote up the Dwarf was, we are told by Mr. Magsman, as Major Tpschoffski—"nobody couldn't pronounce the name," he adds, "and it never was intended anybody should." Corrupted into Chopski by the public, he gets called in the line Chops, partly for that reason, "partly because his real name, if he ever had any real name (which was dubious), was Stakes." Wearing a diamond ring "(or quite as good to look at)" on his forefinger, having the run of his teeth, "and he was a Woodpecker to eat—but all dwarfs are," receiving a good salary, and gathering besides as his perquisites the ha'pence collected by him in a Chaney sarser at the end of every entertainment, the Dwarf never has any money somehow. Nevertheless, having what his admiring proprietor considers "a fine mind, a poetic mind," Mr. Chops indulges himself in the pleasing delusion that one of these days he is to Come Into his Property, his ideas respecting which are never realised by him so powerfully as when he sits upon a barrel-organ and has the handle turned! "Arter the wibration has run through him a little time," says Mr. Magsman, "he screeches out, 'Toby, I feel my property a-coming—gr-r-rind away! I feel the Mint a-jingling in me. I'm a-swelling out into the Bank of England!' Such," reflectively observes his proprietor, "is the influence of music on a poetic mind!" Adding, however, immediately afterwards, "Not that he was partial to any other music but a barrel-organ; on the contrairy, hated it." Indulging in day-dreams about Coming Into his Property and Going Into Society, for which he feels himself formed, and to aspire towards which is his avowed ambition, the mystery, as to where the Dwarf's salary and ha'pence all go, is one day cleared up by his winning a prize in the Lottery, a half-ticket for the twenty-five thousand pounder.

Mr. Chops Comes Into his Property—twelve thousand odd hundred. Further than that, he Goes Into Society "in a chay and four greys with silk jackets." It was at this turning-point in the career of his large-headed but diminutive hero that the grotesque humour of the Reader would play upon the risible nerves of his hearers, as, according to Mr. Disraeli's phrase, Sir Robert Peel used to play upon the House of Commons, "like an old fiddle." Determined to Go Into Society in style, with his twelve thousand odd hundred, Mr. Chops, we are told, "sent for a young man he knowed, as had a very genteel appearance, and was a Bonnet at a gaming-booth. Most respectable brought up," adds Mr. Magsman—"father having been imminent in the livery-stable line, but unfortunate in a commercial crisis through painting a old grey ginger-bay, and sellin' him with a pedigree." In intimate companionship with this Bonnet, "who said his name was Normandy, which it warn't," Mr. Magsman, on invitation by note a little while afterwards, visits Mr. Chops at his lodgings in Pall Mall, London, where he is found carousing not only with the Bonnet but with a third party, of whom we were then told with unconscionable gravity, "When last met, he had on a white Roman shirt, and a bishop's mitre covered with leopard-skin, and played the clarionet all wrong in a band at a Wild Beast Show." How the reverential Magsman, finding the three of them blazing away, blazes away in his turn while remaining in their company, who, that once heard it, has forgotten? "I made the round of the bottles," he says—evidently proud of his achievement—"first separate (to say I had done it), and then mixed 'em altogether (to say I had done it), and then tried two of 'em as half-and-half, and then t'other two; altogether," he adds, "passin' a pleasin' evenin' with a tendency to feel muddled." How all Mr. Chop's blazing away is to terminate everybody but himself perceives clearly enough from the commencement.

Normandy having bolted with the plate, and "him as formerly wore the bishop's mitre" with the jewels, the Dwarf gets out of society by being, as he significantly expresses it, "sold out," and in this plight returns penitently one evening to the show-house of his still-admiring proprietor. Mr. Magsman happens at the moment to be having a dull *tête-à-tête* with a young man without arms, who gets his living by writing with his toes, "which," says the low-spirited narrator, "I had taken on for a month—though he never drawed—except on paper." Hearing a kicking at the street-door, "'Halloa!' I says to the young man, 'what's up?' He rubs his eyebrows with his toes, and he says, 'I can't imagine, Mr. Magsman'—which that young man [with an air of disgust] never *could* imagine nothin', and was monotonous company." Mr. Chops—"I never dropped the 'Mr.' with him," says his again proprietor; "the world might do it, but not me"—eventually dies. Having sat upon the barrel-organ over night, and had the handle turned through all the changes, for the first and only time after his fall, Mr. Chops is found on the following morning, as the disconsolate Magsman expresses it, "gone into much better society than either mine or Pall Mall's." Out of such unpromising materials as these could the alembic of a genius all-embracing in its sympathies extract such an abundance of innocent mirth—an illiterate showman talking to us all the while about such people as the Bonnet of a gaming-booth, or a set of monstrosities he himself has, for a few coppers, on exhibition. Yet, as Mr. Magsman himself remarks rather proudly when commenting on his own establishment, "as for respectability,—if threepence ain't respectable, what is?"

THE POOR TRAVELLER.

APART altogether from the Readings of Charles Dickens, has the reader of this book any remembrance of the original story of "The Poor Traveller"? If he has, he will recognise upon the instant the truth of the words in which we would here speak of it, as of one of those, it may be, slight but exquisite sketches, which are sometimes, in a happy moment, thrown off by the hand of a great master. Comparatively trivial in itself—carelessly dashed off, apparently hap-hazard—having no pretension about it in the least, it is anything, in short, but a finished masterpiece. Yet, for all that, it is marked, here and there, by touches so felicitous and inimitable in their way, that we hardly find the like in the artist's more highly elaborated and ambitious productions. Not that one would speak of it, however, as of a drawing upon toned paper in neutral tint, or as of a picture pencilled in sepia or with crayons; one would rather liken it to a radiant water-colour, chequered with mingled storm and sunshine, sparkling with lifelike effects, and glowing with brilliancy. And yet the little work is one, when you come to look into it, that is but the product of a seemingly artless *abandon,* in which without an effort the most charming results have been arrived at, obviously upon the instant, and quite unerringly.

Trudging down to Chatham, footsore and without a farthing in his pocket, it is in this humble guise first of all that he comes before us, this Poor Traveller. Christian name, Richard, better known as Dick, his own surname dropped upon the road, he assumes that of Doubledick--being thenceforth spoken of all through the tale, even to the very end of it, by his new name, as Richard Doubledick. A scapegrace, a ne'er-do-well, an incorrigible, hopeless of himself, despaired of by others, he has "gone wrong and run wild." His heart, still in the right place, has been sealed up. "Betrothed to a good and beautiful girl whom he had loved better than she—or perhaps even he—believed," he had given her cause, in an evil hour, to tell him solemnly that she would never marry any other man; that she would live single for his sake, but that her lips, "that Mary Marshall's lips," would never address another word to him on earth, bidding him in the end —Go! and Heaven forgive him! Hence, in point of fact, this journey of his on foot down to Chatham, for the purpose of enlisting, if possible, in a cavalry regiment, his object being to get shot, though he himself thinks in his devil-may-care indifference, that "he might as well ride to death as be at the trouble of walking." Premising simply that his hero's age is at this time twenty-two, and his height five foot ten, and that, there being no cavalry at the moment in Chatham, he enlists into a regiment of the line, where he is glad to get drunk and forget all about it, the Author readily made the path clear for the opening up of his narrative.

Whenever Charles Dickens introduced this tale among his Readings, how beautifully he related it! After recounting how Private Doubledick was clearly going to the dogs, associating himself with the dregs of every regiment, seldom being sober and constantly under punishment, until it became plain at last to the whole barracks that very soon indeed he would come to be flogged, when the Reader came at this point to the words—"Now the captain of Doubledick's company was a young gentleman not above five years his senior, whose eyes had an expression in them which affected Private Doubledick in a very remarkable way"—the effect was singularly striking. Out of the Reader's own eyes would look the eyes of that Captain, as the Author himself describes them: "They were bright, handsome, dark eyes, what are called laughing eyes generally, and, when serious, rather steady than severe." But, he immediately went on to say, they were the only eyes then left in his narrowed world that could not be met without a sense of shame by Private Doubledick. Insomuch that if he observed Captain Taunton coming towards him, even when he himself was most callous and unabashed, "he would rather turn back and go any distance out of the way, than encounter those two handsome, dark, bright eyes." Here it was that came, what many will still vividly remember, as one of the most exquisitely portrayed incidents in the whole of this Reading—the interview between Captain Taunton and Private Doubledick!

The latter, having passed forty-eight hours in the Black Hole, has been just summoned, to his great dismay, to the Captain's quarters. Having about him all the squalor of his incarceration, he shrinks from making his appearance before one whose silent gaze even was a reproach. However, not being so mad yet as to disobey orders, he goes up to the officers' quarters immediately upon his release from the Black Hole, twisting and breaking in his hands as he goes along a bit of the straw that had formed its decorative furniture.

"'Come in!'

"Private Doubledick pulled off his cap, took a stride forward and stood in the light of the dark bright eyes."

From that moment until the end of the interview, the two men alternately were standing there distinctly before the audience upon the platform.

"Doubledick! do you know where you are going to?"

"To the devil, sir!"

"Yes, and very fast."

Thereupon one did not hear the words simply, one saw it done precisely as it is described in the original narrative: "Private Richard Doubledick turned the straw of the Black Hole in his mouth and made a *miserable* salute of acquiescence." Captain Taunton then remonstrates with him thus earnestly: "Doubledick, since I entered his Majesty's service, a boy of seventeen, I have been pained to see many men of promise going that road; but I have never been *so* pained to see a man determined to make the shameful journey, as I have been, ever since you joined the regiment, to see *you*." At this point in the printed story, as it was originally penned, one reads that "Private Richard Doubledick began to find a film stealing over the floor at which he looked; also to find the legs of the Captain's breakfast-table turning crooked as if he saw them through water." Although those words are erased in the reading copy, and were not uttered, pretty nearly the effect of them was visible when, after a momentary pause, the disheartened utterance was faltered out—

"I am only a common soldier, sir. It signifies very little what such a poor brute comes to."

In answer to the next remonstrance from his officer, Doubledick's words are blurted out yet more despairingly—

"I hope to get shot soon, sir, and then the regiment, and the world together, will be rid of me!"

What are the descriptive words immediately following this in the printed narrative? They also were visibly expressed upon the platform. "Looking up he met the eyes that had so strong an influence over him. He put his hand before his own eyes, and the breast of his disgrace-jacket swelled as if it would fly asunder." His observant adviser thereupon quietly but very earnestly remarks, that he would rather see this in him (Doubledick) than he would see five thousand guineas counted out upon the table between them for a gift to his (the Captain's) good mother," adding suddenly, "Have you a mother?" Doubledick is thankful to say she is dead. Reminded by the Captain that if his praises were sounded from mouth to mouth through the whole regiment, through the whole army, through the whole country, he would wish she had lived to say with pride and joy, "He is my son!" Doubledick cries out, "Spare me, sir! She would never have heard any good of me. She would never have had any pride or joy in owning herself my mother. Love and compassion she might have had, and would always have had, I know; but not—spare me, sir! I am a broken wretch quite at your mercy."

By this time, according to the words of the writing, according only to the eloquent action of the Reading, "He had turned his face to the wall and stretched out his *imploring* hand." How eloquently that "imploring hand" spoke in the agonised, dumb supplication of its movement, coupled as it was with the shaken frame and the averted countenance, those who witnessed this Reading will readily recall to their recollection. As also the emotion expressed in the next broken utterances exchanged by the interlocutors:—

"My friend——"

"God bless you, sir!"

Captain Taunton, interrupted for the moment, adding—

"You are at the crisis of your fate, my friend. Hold your course unchanged a little longer, and you know what must happen. *I* know better than ever you can imagine, that after that has happened you are a lost man. No man who could shed such tears could bear such marks."

Doubledick, replying in a low shivering voice, "I fully believe it, sir," the young Captain adds—

"But a man in any station can do his duty, and in doing it can earn his own respect, even if his case should be so very unfortunate and so very rare, that he can earn no other man's. A common soldier, poor brute though you called him just now, has this advantage in the stormy times we live in, that he always does his duty before a host of sympathising witnesses. Do you doubt that he may so do it as to be extolled through a whole regiment, through a whole army, through a whole country? Turn while you may yet retrieve the past and try."

With a nearly bursting heart Richard cries out, "I will! I ask but one witness, sir!" The reply is instant and significant, "I understand you. I will be a watchful and a faithful one." It is a compact between them, a compact sealed and ratified. "I have heard from Private Doubledick's own lips," said the narrator, and in tones how manly and yet how tender in their vibration, "that he dropped down upon his knee, kissed that officer's hand, arose, and went out of the light of the dark bright eyes, an altered man." From the date to them both of this memorable interview he followed the two hither and thither among the battle-fields of the great war between England in coalition with the other nations of Europe and Napoleon.

Wherever Captain Taunton led, there, "close to him, ever at his side, firm as a rock, true as the sun, brave as Mars," would for certain be found that famous soldier Sergeant Doubledick. As Sergeant-Major the latter is shown, later on, upon one desperate occasion cutting his way single-handed through a mass of men, recovering the colours of his regiment, and rescuing his wounded Captain from the very jaws of death "in a jungle of horses' hoofs and sabres"—for which deed of gallantry and all but desperation, he is forthwith raised from the ranks, appearing no longer as a non-commissioned officer, but as Ensign Doubledick. At last, one fatal day in the trenches, during the siege of Badajos, Major Taunton and Ensign Doubledick find themselves hurrying forward against a party of French infantry. At this juncture, at the very moment when Doubledick sees the officer at the head of the enemy's soldiery—"a courageous, handsome, gallant officer of five-and-thirty"—waving his sword, and with an eager and excited cry rallying his men, they fire, and Major Taunton has dropped. The encounter closing within ten minutes afterwards on the arrival of assistance to the two Englishmen, "the best friend man ever had" is laid upon a coat spread out upon the wet clay by the heart-riven subaltern, whom years before his generous counsel had rescued from ignominious destruction. Three little spots of blood are visible on the shirt of Major Taunton as he lies there with the breast of his uniform opened.

"Dear Doubledick,—I am dying."

"For the love of Heaven, no! Taunton! My preserver, my guardian angel, my witness! Dearest, truest, kindest of human beings! Taunton! For God's sake!"

To listen to that agonised entreaty as it started from the trembling and one could almost have fancied whitened lips of the Reader, was to be with him there upon the instant on the far-off battle-field. Taunton dies "with his hand upon the breast in which he had revived a soul." Doubledick, prostrated and inconsolable in his bereavement, has but two cares seemingly for the rest of his existence—one to preserve a packet of hair to be given to the mother of the friend lost to him; the other, to encounter that French officer who had rallied the men under whose fire that friend had fallen. "A new legend," quoth the narrator, "now began to incubate among our troops; and it was, that when he and the French officer came face to face once more, there would be weeping in France." Failing to meet him, however, through all the closing scenes of the great war, Doubledick, by this time promoted to his lieutenancy, follows the old regimental colours, ragged, scarred, and riddled with shot, through the fierce conflicts of Quatre Bras and Ligny, falling at last desperately wounded—all but dead—upon the field of Waterloo.

How, having been tenderly nursed during the total eclipse of an appallingly lengthened period of unconsciousness, he wakes up at last in Brussels to find that during a little more than momentary and at first an utterly forgotten interval of his stupor, he has been married to the gentle-handed nurse who has been all the while in attendance upon him, and who is no other, of course, than his faithful first love, Mary Marshall! How, returning homewards, an invalided hero, Captain Doubledick becomes, in a manner, soon afterwards, the adopted son of Major Taunton's mother! How the latter, having gone, some time later, on a visit to a French family near Aix, is followed by her other son, her other self, he has almost come to be, "now a hardy, handsome man in the full vigour of life," on his receiving from the head of the house a gracious and courtly invitation for "the honour of the company of cet homme si justement célèbre, Monsieur le Capitaine Richard Doubledick!" These were among the incidents in due sequence immediately afterwards recounted!

Arriving at the old château upon a fête-day, when the household are scattered abroad in the gardens and shrubberies at their rejoicings, Captain Doubledick passes through the open porch into the lofty stone hall. There, being a total stranger, he is almost scared by the intrusive clanking of his boots. Suddenly he starts back, feeling his face turn white! For, in the gallery looking down at him, is the French officer whose picture he has carried in his mind so long and so far. The latter, disappearing in another instant for the staircase, enters directly afterwards with a bright sudden look upon his countenance, "Such a look as it had worn in that fatal moment," so well and so terribly remembered! All this was portrayed with startling vividness by the Author of the little sketch in his capacity as the sympathetic realizer of the dreams of his own imagination.

Exquisite was the last glimpse of the delineation, when the Captain—after many internal revulsions of feeling, while he gazes through the window of the bed-chamber allotted to him in the old château, "whence he could see the smiling prospect and the peaceful vineyards"—thinks musingly to himself, "Spirit of my departed friend, is it through thee these better thoughts are rising in my mind! Is it thou who hast shown me, all the way

I have been drawn to meet this man, the blessings of the altered time! Is it thou who hast sent thy stricken mother to me, to stay my angry hand! Is it from thee the whisper comes, that this man only did his duty as thou didst—and as I did through thy guidance, which saved me, here on earth—and that he did no more!"

Then it was, we were told, there came to him the second and crowning resolution of his life: "That neither to the French officer, nor to the mother of his departed friend, nor to any soul while either of the two was living, would he breathe what only *he* knew." Then it was that the author perfected his Reading by the simple utterance of its closing words—"And when he touched that French officer's glass with his own that day at dinner, he secretly forgave him—forgave him in the name of the Divine Forgiver." With a moral no less noble and affecting, no less grand and elevating than this, the lovely idyll closed. The final glimpse of the scene at the old Aix château was like the view of a sequestered orchard through the ivied porchway of a village church. The concluding words of the prelection were like the sound of the organ voluntary at twilight, when the worshippers are dispersing.

MRS. GAMP.

A whimsical and delightful recollection comes back to the writer of these pages at the moment of inscribing as the title of this Reading the name of the preposterous old lady who is the real heroine of "Martin Chuzzlewit." It is the remembrance of Charles Dickens's hilarious enjoyment of a casual jest thrown out, upon his having incidentally mentioned — as conspicuous among the shortcomings of the first acting version of that story upon the boards of the Lyceum—the certainly surprising fact that Mrs. Gamp's part, as originally set down for Keeley, had not a single "which" in it. "Why, it ought actually to have begun with one!" was the natural exclamation of the person he was addressing, who added instantly, with affected indignation, "Not one? Why, next they'll be playing Macbeth without the Witches!" The joyous laugh with which this ludicrous conceit was greeted by the Humorist, still rings freshly and musically in our remembrance. And the recollection of it is doubtless all the more vivid because of the mirthful retrospect having relation to one of the most recent of Dickens's blithe home dinners in his last town residence immediately before his hurried return to Gad's Hill in the summer of 1870. Although we were happily with him afterwards, immediately before the time came when we could commune with him no more, the occasion referred to is one in which we recall him to mind as he was when we saw him last at his very gayest, radiant with that sense of enjoyment which it was his especial delight to diffuse around him throughout his life so abundantly.

Among all his humorous creations, Mrs. Gamp is perhaps the most intensely original and the most thoroughly individualised. She is not only a creation of character, she is in herself a creator of character. To the Novelist we are indebted for Mrs. Gamp, but to Mrs. Gamp herself we are indebted for Mrs. Harris. That most mythical of all imaginary beings is certainly quite unique; she is strictly, as one may say, *sui generis* in the whole world of fiction. A figment born from a figment; one fancy evolved from another; the shadow of a shadow. If only in remembrance of that one daring adumbration from Mrs. Gamp's inner consciousness, that purely supposititious entity "which her name, I'll not deceive you, is Harris," one would say that Mr. Mould, the undertaker, has full reason for exclaiming, in regard to Mrs. Gamp, "I'll tell you what, that's a woman whose intellect is immensely superior to her station in life. That's a woman who observes and reflects in a wonderful manner." Mr. Mould becomes so strongly impressed at last with a sense of her exceptional merits, that in a deliciously ludicrous outburst of professional generosity he caps the climax of his eulogium by observing, "She's the sort of woman, now, that one would almost feel disposed to bury for nothing—and do it neatly, too!" Thoroughly akin, by the way, to which exceedingly questionable expression of goodwill on the part of Mr. Mould, is Mrs. Gamp's equally confiding outburst of philanthropy from *her* point of view, where she remarks—of course to her familiar, as Socrates when communing with his Dæmon—"'Mrs. Harris,' I says to her, 'don't name the charge, for if I could afford to lay my fellow-creeturs out for nothink, I would gladly do it, sich is the love I bears 'em.'"

A benevolent unbosoming, or self-revelation, that last, on the part of Mrs. Gamp, so astoundingly outspoken of its kind, that it forces upon one, in regard to her whole character, the almost inevitable reflection that her grotesque and inexhaustible humour, like Falstaff's irrepressible and exhilarating wit, redeems what would be otherwise in itself utterly irredeemable. For, as commentators have remarked, in regard to Shakspere's Fat Knight, that Sir John is an unwieldy mass of every conceivable bad quality, being, among other things, a liar, a coward, a drunkard, a braggart, a cheat, and a debauchee, one might bring, if not an equally formidable, certainly an equally lengthened, indictment against the whole character of Mrs. Gamp, justifying the validity of each disreputable charge upon the testimony of her own evidence.

In its way, the impersonation of Mrs. Gamp by her creator was nearly as surprising as his original delineation of her in his capacity as Novelist. Happily, to bring out the finer touches of the humorous in her portraiture, there were repeated asides in the Reading, added to which other contrasting characters were here and there momentarily introduced. Mr. Pecksniff—hardly recognisable, by the way, *as* Mr. Pecksniff—took part, but a very subordinate part, in the conversation, as did Mr. Mould also, and as, towards the close of it, likewise did Mrs. Prig of Bartlemy's. But, monopolist though Mrs. Gamp showed herself to be in her manner of holding forth, her talk never degenerated into a monologue.

Mr. Pecksniff setting forth in a hackney cabriolet to arrange, on behalf of Jonas Chuzzlewit, for the funeral of the latter's father, in regard to which he is enjoined to spare no expense, arrives, in due course, in Kingsgate-street, High Holborn, in quest of the female functionary—"a nurse and watcher, and performer of nameless offices about the dead, whom the undertaker had recommended." His destination is reached when he stands face to face with the lady's lodging over the bird-fancier's, "next door but one to the celebrated mutton-pie shop, and directly opposite to the original cats'-meat warehouse." Here Mr. Pecksniff's performance upon the knocker naturally arouses the whole neighbourhood, it, the knocker, being so ingeniously constructed as to wake the street with ease, without making the smallest impression upon the premises to which it was addressed. Everybody is at once under the impression that, as a matter of course, he is "upon an errand touching not the close of life, but the other end"—the married ladies, especially, crying out with uncommon interest, "Knock at the winder, sir, knock at the winder! Lord bless you, don't lose no more time than you can help,—knock at the winder!" Mrs. Gamp herself, when roused, is under the same embarrassing misapprehension. Immediately, however, Mr. Pecksniff has explained the object of his mission, Mrs. Gamp, who has a face for all occasions, thereupon putting on her mourning countenance, the surrounding matrons, while rating her visitor roundly, signify that they would be glad to know what he means by terrifying delicate females with "his corpses!" The unoffending gentleman eventually, after hustling Mrs. Gamp into the cabriolet, drives off "overwhelmed with popular execration."

Here it is that Mrs. Gamp's distinctive characteristics begin to assert themselves conspicuously. Her labouring under the most erroneous impressions as to the conveyance in which she is travelling, evidently confounding it with mail-coaches, insomuch that, in regard to her luggage, she clamours to the driver to "put it in the boot," her absorbing anxiety about the pattens, "with which she plays innumerable games of quoits upon Mr. Pecksniff's legs," her evolutions in that confined space with her most prominently visible chattel, "a species of gig umbrella," prepare the way for her still more characteristic confidences. Then in earnest—she had spoken twice before that from her window over the bird-fancier's—but then in earnest, on their approaching the house of mourning, her voice, in the Reading, became recognisable. A voice snuffy, husky, unctuous, the voice of a fat old woman, one so fat that she is described in the book as having had a difficulty in looking over herself—a voice, as we read elsewhere in the novel, having borne upon the breeze about it a peculiar flagrance, "as if a passing fairy had hiccoughed, and had previously been to a wine-vaults."

"'And so the gentleman's dead, sir! Ah! the more's the pity!'—(*She didn't even know his name.*)—'But it's as certain as being born, except that we can't make our calc'lations as exact. Ah, dear!'"

Simply to hear those words uttered by the Reader—especially the interjected words above italicised—was to have a relish of anticipation at once for all that followed. Mrs. Gamp's pathetic allusion, immediately afterwards, to her recollection of the time "when Gamp was summonsed to his long home," and when she "see him a-laying in the hospital with a penny-piece on each eye, and his wooden leg under his left arm," not only confirmed the delighted impression of the hearers as to their having her there before them in her identity, but was the signal for the roars of laughter that, rising and falling in volume all through the Reading, terminated only some time after its completion.

Immediately after came the first introduction by her of the name of Mrs. Harris. "At this point," observed the narrator, "she was fain to stop for breath. And," he went on directly to remark, with a combination of candour and seriousness that were in themselves irresistibly ludicrous, "advantage may be taken of the circumstance to state that a fearful mystery surrounded this lady of the name of Harris, whom no one in the circle of Mrs. Gamp's acquaintance had ever seen; neither did any human being know her place of residence—the prevalent opinion being that she was a phantom of Mrs. Gamp's brain, created for the purpose of holding complimentary dialogues with her on all manner of subjects." Eminently seasonable, as a preliminary flourish in this way, is the tribute paid by her to Mrs. Gamp's abstemiousness, on the understanding that is, that the latter's one golden rule of life, is complied with—" 'Leave the bottle on the chimbley-piece, and don't ast me to take none, but let me put my lips to it when I am so dispoged, and then, Mrs. Harris, I says, I will do what I am engaged to, according to the best of my ability.' 'Mrs. Gamp,' she says, in answer, 'if ever there was a sober creetur to be got at eighteenpence a day for working people, and three-and-six for gentlefolks,—night-watching being a extra charge,—

you are that inwallable person. Never did I think, till I know'd you, as any woman could sick-nurse and monthly likeways, on the little that you takes to drink.' 'Mrs. Harris, ma'am,' I says to her, 'none on us knows what we can do till we tries; and wunst *I* thought so too. But now,' I says, 'my half a pint of porter fully satisfies; perwisin', Mrs. Harris, that it's brought reg'lar, and draw'd mild.'" Not but occasionally even that modest "sip of liquor" she finds so far "settling heavy on the chest" as to necessitate, every now and then, a casual dram by way of extra quencher.

It was so arranged in the Reading that, immediately upon the completion of Mrs. Gamp's affecting narrative of the confidential opinions of her sobriety entertained by Mrs. Harris, Mr. Mould, the undertaker, opportunely presented to the audience his well-remembered countenance—"a face in which a queer attempt at melancholy was at odds with a smirk of satisfaction." The impersonation, here, was conveyed in something better than the unsatisfactory hint by which that attempted in regard to Mr. Pecksniff was alone to be expressed. Speaking of Old Chuzzlewit's funeral, as ordered by his bereaved son, Mr. Jonas, with "no limitation, positively no limitation in point of expense," the undertaker observes to Mr. Pecksniff, "This is one of the most impressive cases, sir, that I have seen in the whole course of my professional experience. Anything so filial as this—anything so honourable to human nature, anything *so* expensive, anything so calculated to reconcile all of us to the world we live in—never yet came under my observation. It only proves, sir, what was so forcibly expressed by the lamented poet,—buried at Stratford,—that there is good in everything." Even the very manner of his departure was delicious: "Mr. Mould was going away with a brisk smile, when he remembered the occasion," we read in the narrative and saw on the platform. "Quickly becoming depressed again, he sighed; looked into the crown of his hat, as if for comfort; put it on without finding any; and slowly departed."

The spirit and substance of the whole Reading, however, were, as a matter of course, Mrs. Gamp and her grotesque remembrances, drawn, these latter from the inexhaustible fund of her own personal and mostly domestic experiences. "Although the blessing of a daughter," she observed, in one of her confiding retrospects, "was deniged me, which, if we had had one, Gamp would certainly have drunk its little shoes right off its feet, as with one precious boy he did, and arterwards sent the child a errand to sell his wooden leg for any liquor it would fetch as matches in the rough; which was truly done beyond his years, for ev'ry individgle penny that child lost at tossing for kidney pies, and come home arterwards quite bold, to break the news, and offering to drown'd himself if such would be a satisfaction to his parents." At another moment, when descanting upon all her children collectively in one of her faithfully reported addresses to her familiar: "'My own family,' I says, 'has fallen out of three-pair backs, and had damp door-steps settled on their lungs, and one was turned up smilin' in a bedstead unbeknown. And as to husbands, there's a wooden leg gone likeways home to its account, which in its constancy of walking into public-'ouses, and never coming out again till fetched by force, was quite as weak as flesh, if not weaker."

Somehow, when those who were assisting at this Reading, as the phrase is, had related to them the manner in which Mrs. Gamp entered on her official duties in the sick chamber, they appeared to be assisting also at her toilette: as, for example, when "she put on a yellow nightcap of prodigious size, in shape resembling a cabbage, having previously divested herself of a row of bald old curls, which could scarcely be called false they were so innocent of anything approaching to deception." One missed sadly at this point in the later version of this Reading what was included in her first conversation on the door-mat as to her requirements for supper enumerated after this fashion, "in tones expressive of faintness," to the housemaid: "I think, young woman, as I could peck a little bit of pickled salmon, with a little sprig of fennel and a sprinkling o' white pepper. I takes new bread, my dear, with jest a little pat o' fredge butter and a mossel o' cheese. With respect to ale, if they draws the Brighton Tipper at any 'ouse nigh here,

I takes that ale at night, my love; not as I cares for it myself, but on accounts of its being considered wakeful by the doctors; and whatever you do, young woman, don't bring me more than a shilling's worth of gin-and-water, warm, when I rings the bell a second time; for that is always my allowange, and I never takes a drop beyond. In case there should be sich a thing as a cowcumber in the 'ouse, I'm rather partial to 'em, though I am but a poor woman." Winding all up,—with one of those amazing confusions of a Scriptural recollection which prompts her at another time in the novel to exclaim, in regard to the Ankworks package, "'I wish it was in Jonadge's belly, I do,' appearing to confound the prophet with the whale in that mysterious aspiration,"—by observing at this point, "Rich folks may ride on camels, but it ain't so easy for 'em to see out of a needle's eye. That is my comfort, and I hope I knows it." One whole chapter of "Martin Chuzzlewit," with the exception of the merest fragment of it—*the* chapter pre-eminently in relation to Mrs. Gamp—we always regretted as having been either overlooked or purposely set aside in the compilation both of the earlier and the later version of this Reading, the chapter, that is, in which Mrs. Gamp and Mrs. Prig converse together in the former's sleeping apartment.

The mere description of the interior of that chamber, related by the Author's lips, would have been so irresistibly ridiculous—the tent bedstead ornamented with pippins carved in timber, that tumbled down on the slightest provocation like a wooden shower-bath—the chest of drawers, from which the handles had long been pulled off, so that its contents could only be got at either by tilting the whole structure until all the drawers fell out together, or by opening each of them singly with knives like oysters—the miscellaneous salad bought for twopence by Betsey Prig on condition that the vendor could get it all into her pocket (including among other items a green vegetable of an expansive nature, of such magnificent proportions that before it could be got either in or out it had to be shut up like an umbrella), which was happily accomplished in High Holborn, to the breathless interest of a hackney-coach stand.

One inestimable portion, however, of this memorable occasion of festivity between those frequend pardners, Betsey Prig and Sairey Gamp, was, by a most ingenious dovetailing together of two disjointed parts, incorporated with the adroitly compacted materials of a Reading that was as brief as the laughter provoked by it was boisterous and inextinguishable. As to the manner of the dovetailing, it will be readily recalled to recollection. Immediately upon Mrs. Gamp's awaking at the close of her night watch, we were told that Mrs. Prig relieved punctually, but that she relieved in an ill temper. "The best among us have their failings, and it must be conceded of Mrs. Prig," observed the Reader with a hardly endurable gravity of explanation, "that if there were a blemish in the goodness of her disposition, it was a habit she had of not bestowing all its sharp and acid properties upon her patients (as a thoroughly amiable woman would have done), but of keeping a considerable remainder for the service of her friends." Looking offensively at Mrs. Gamp, and winking her eye, as Mrs. Prig does immediately upon her entrance, it is felt by the former to be necessary that Betsey should at once be made sensible of her exact station in society; wherefore Mrs. Gamp prefaced a remonstrance with—

"Mrs. Harris, Betsey ——"

"Bother Mrs. Harris!"

Then it was that the Reader added:—

"Mrs. Gamp looked at Betsey with amazement, incredulity, and indignation. Mrs. Prig, winking her eye tighter, folded her arms and uttered these tremendous words:—

"'I don't believe there's no sich a person!'

"With these expressions, she snapped her fingers, once, twice, thrice, each time nearer to Mrs. Gamp, and then turned away as one who felt that there was now a gulf between them that nothing could ever bridge across."

The most comic of all the Readings closed thus abruptly with a roar.

BOOTS AT THE HOLLY TREE INN.

Even the immortal Boots at the White Hart, Borough, who was first revealed to us in a coarse striped waistcoat with black calico sleeves and blue glass buttons, drab breeches and gaiters, and who answered to the name of Sam, would not, we are certain, have disdained to have been put in friendly relations with Cobbs, as one in every way worthy of his companionship. The Boots at the Holly Tree Inn, though more lightly sketched, was quite as much of an original creation in his way as that other Christmas friend of ours, the warm-hearted and loquacious Cheap Jack, Doctor Marigold. And each of those worthies, it should be added, had really about him an equal claim to be regarded, as an original creation, as written, or as impersonated by the Author. As a character orally portrayed, Cobbs was fully on a par with Doctor Marigold. Directly the Reader opened his lips, whether as the Boots or as the Cheap Jack, the Novelist seemed to disappear, and there instead, talking glibly to us from first to last just as the case might happen to be, was either the patterer on the cart footboard or honest Cobbs touching his hair with a bootjack. His very first words not only lead up to his confidences, but in the same breath struck the key-note of his character. "Where had he been? Lord, everywhere! What had he been? Bless you, everything a'most. Seen a good deal? Why, of course he had. Would be easier for him to tell what he hadn't seen than what he had. Ah! A deal, it would. What was the curiosest thing he'd seen? Well! He didn't know—couldn't name it momently—unless it was a Unicorn, and he see *him* over at a Fair. But"—and here came the golden retrospect, a fairy tale of love told by a tavern Boots, and told all through, moreover, as none but a Boots could tell it—"Supposing a young gentleman not eight year old, was to run away with a fine young woman of seven, might I think *that* a queer start? Certainly! Then, that was a start as he himself had had his blessed eyes on—and he'd cleaned the shoes they run away in—and they was so little he couldn't get his hand into 'em." Whereupon, following up the thread of his discourse, Boots would take his crowd of hearers, quite willingly on their part, into the heart of the charming labyrinth.

The descriptive powers of Cobbs, it will be admitted, were for one thing very remarkable. Master Harry Walmers' father, for instance, he hits off to a nicety in a phrase or two. "He was a gentleman of spirit, and good looking, and held his head up when he walked, and had what you may call Fire about him:" adding, that he wrote poetry, rode, ran, cricketed, danced and acted, and "done it all equally beautiful." Another and a very significant touch, by the way, was imparted to that same portraiture later on, just, in point of fact before the close of Cobbs's reminiscence, and one so lightly given that it was conveyed through a mere passing parenthesis—namely, where the young father was described by Boots as standing beside Master Harry Walmers' bed, in the Holly Tree Inn, looking down at the little sleeping face, "looking wonderfully like it," says Cobbs, who adds, "(they do say as he ran away with Mrs. Walmers)." Although Boots described Master Harry's father from the first as "uncommon proud of him, as his only child, you see," the worthy fellow took especial care at once to add, that "he didn't spoil him neither." Having a will of his own, and a eye of his own, and being one that would be minded, while he never tired of hearing the fine bright boy "sing his songs about Young May Moons is beaming, love, and When he who adores thee has left but the name, and that: still," said Boots, "he kept the command over the child, and the child *was* a child, and it's very much to be wished more of 'em was." At the particular period referred to in this portion of his narrative, Boots informed us pleasantly, that he came to know all about it by reason of his being in his then capacity as Mr. Walmers' under-gardener, always about in the summer time, near the windows, on the lawn "a-mowing and sweeping, and weeding and pruning, and this and that"—with his eyes and ears open, of course, we may presume, in a manner befitting his intelligence.

Perhaps, there was after all nothing better in the delivery of the whole of this Reading, than the utterance of the two words italicised below in the first dialogue, reported by Boots as having taken place between himself and Master Harry Walmers, junior, when "that mite," as Boots calls him, stops one day, along with the fine young woman of seven already mentioned, where Boots (then under-gardener, remember) was hoeing weeds in the gravel:—

"'Cobbs,' he says, 'I like *you.*' 'Do you, sir? I'm proud to hear it.' 'Yes, I do, Cobbs. Why do I like you, do you think, Cobbs?' 'Don't know, Master Harry, I'm sure.' 'Because Norah likes you, Cobbs.' 'Indeed, sir? That's very gratifying.' 'Gratifying, Cobbs? It is better than millions of the brightest diamonds, to be liked by Norah?' '*Certainly, sir.*'"

Confirmed naturally enough in his good opinion of Cobbs by this thorough community of sentiment, Master Harry, who has been given to understand from the latter that he is going to leave, and, further than that, on inquiring, that he wouldn't object to another situation "if it was a good 'un," observes, while tucking that other mite in her little sky-blue mantle under his arm, "Then, Cobbs, you shall be our head gardener when we are married." Boots, thereupon, in the person of the Reader, went on to describe how "the babies with their long bright curling hair, their sparkling eyes, and their beautiful light tread, rambled about the garden deep in love," sometimes here, sometimes there, always under his own sympathetic and admiring observation, until one day, down by the pond, he heard Master Harry say, "Adorable Norah, kiss me and say you love me to distraction." Altogether Cobbs seemed exactly, and with delicious humour, to define the entire situation when he declared, that "on the whole the contemplation of them two babies had a tendency to make him feel as if he was in love himself—only he didn't know who with!"

The delightful gravity of countenance (with a covert sparkle in the eye where the daintiest indications of fun were given by the Reader) lent a charm of its own to the merest nothing, comparatively, in the whimsical dialogues he was reporting. Master Harry, for example, having confided to Cobbs one evening, when the latter was watering the flowers, that he was going on a visit to his grandmama at York—"'Are you indeed, sir? I hope you'll have a pleasant time. I'm going into Yorkshire myself, when I leave here.' 'Are you going to your grandmama's, Cobbs?' 'No, sir. I haven't got such a thing.' 'Not as a grandmama, Cobbs?' 'No, sir.'" Immediately after which, on the boy observing to his humble confidant, that he shall be so glad to go because "Norah's going," Cobbs, naturally enough, as it seemed, took occasion to remark, "You'll be all right then, sir, with your beautiful sweetheart by your side." Whereupon we realised more clearly than ever the delicate whimsicality of the whole delineation, when we saw, as well as heard, the boy return a-flushing, "Cobbs, I never let anybody joke about that when I can prevent them," Cobbs immediately explaining in all humility, "It wasn't a joke, sir—wasn't so meant." No wonder, Boots had exclaimed previously: "And the courage of that boy! Bless you, he'd have throwed off his little hat and tucked up his little sleeves and gone in at a lion, he would—if they'd happened to meet one, and she [Norah] had been frightened." At the close of Boots's record of this last-quoted conversation with Master Harry, came one of the drollest touches in the Reading—"'Cobbs,' says that boy, 'I'll tell you a secret. At Norah's house, they have been joking her about me, and [with a wondering look] pretending to laugh at our being engaged! Pretending to make game of it, Cobbs!' 'Such, sir,' I says, 'is the depravity of human natur.'" A glance during the utterance of which words, either at the Reader himself or at his audience, was something enjoyable.

Hardly less inspiriting in its way was the incidental mention, directly after this by Cobbs, of the manner in which he gave Mr. Walmers notice, not that he'd anything to complain of—"'Thanking you, sir, I find myself as well sitiwated here as I could hope to be anywheres. The truth is, sir, that I'm a going to seek my fortun.' 'O, indeed, Cobbs?' he says, 'I hope you may find it.'" Boots hereupon giving his audience the assurance, with the characteristic touch of the boot-jack to his forehead, that "he hadn't found it yet!"

Then came the delectable account of the elopement—full, true, and particular—from the veracious lips of Cobbs himself, at that time, and again some years afterwards, when he came to call up his recollections, Boots at the Holly Tree Inn. Passages here and there in his description of the incident were irrisistibly laughable. Master Harry's going down to the old lady's in York, for example, "which old lady were so wrapt up in that child as she would have give that child the teeth in her head (if she had had any)." The arrival of "them two children," again at the Holly Tree Inn, he, as bold as brass, tucking her in her little sky-blue mantle under his arm, with the memorable dinner order, "Chops and cherry pudding for two!" Their luggage, even, when gravely enumerated—the lady having "a parasol, a smelling bottle, a round and a half of cold buttered toast, eight peppermint drops, and a doll's hair-brush;" the gentleman having "about half a dozen yards of string, a knife, three or four sheets of writing paper folded up surprisingly small, a orange, and a chaney mug with his name on it." Several of the little chance phrases, the merest atoms of exclamation here and there, will still be borne in mind as having had an intense flavour of fun about them, as syllabled in the Reading. Boots's "Sir, to you," when his governor, the hotel-keeper, proposes to run over to York to quiet their friends' minds, while Cobbs keeps his eye upon the innocents! Master Harry's replying to Boots' suggestion, that they should wile away the time by a walk down Love-lane—"'Get out with you, Cobbs!'—that was that there boy's expression." The glee of the children was prettily told too on their finding "Good Cobbs! Dear Cobbs!" among the strangers around them at their temporary halting-place. They themselves appearing smaller than ever in his eyes, by reason of his finding them "with their little legs entirely off the ground, of course—and it really is not possible to express how small them children looked!—on a e-normous sofa;" immense at any time, but looking like a Great Bed of Ware then by comparison.

How, during the governor's absence in search of their friends, Cobbs, feeling himself all the while to be "the meanest rascal for deceiving 'em, that ever was born," gets up a cock and a bull story about a pony he's acquainted with, who'll take them on nicely to Gretna Green—but who was not at liberty the first day, and the next was only "half clipped, you see, and couldn't be took out in that state for fear it should strike to his inside"—was related with the zest of one who had naturally the keenest relish possible for every humorous particular. Finding the lady in tears one time when Boots goes to see how the runaway couple are getting on, "Mrs. Harry Walmers, junior, fatigued, sir?" asks Cobbs. "Yes, she is tired, Cobbs; but she is not used to be away from home, and she has been in low spirits again. Cobbs, do you think you could bring a biffin, please?"—"I ask your pardon, sir, What was it you ——?" "I think a Norfolk biffin would rouse her, Cobbs." Restoratives of that kind, Boots would seem to have regarded as too essential to Mrs. Harry Walmers junior's happiness. Hence, when he comes upon the pair over their dinner of "biled fowl and bread-and-butter pudding," Boots privately owns that "he could have wished to have seen her more sensible to the woice of love, and less abandoning of herself to the currants in the pudding." According to Cobbs's own account of the gentleman, however, it should be added that *he* too could play his part very effectively at table, for—having mentioned another while, how the two of them had ordered overnight sweet milk-and-water and toast and currant jelly for breakfast—when Cobbs comes upon them the next morning at their meal, he describes Master Harry as sitting behind his breakfast cup "a tearing away at the jelly as if he had been his own father!"

Remorseful in the thought of betraying them, Boots at one moment declared, that rather than combine any longer against them, he would by preference have had it out in half-a-dozen rounds with the governor!" And at another time, when the said governor had returned from York, "with Mr. Walmers and a elderly lady," Boots, while conducting Mr. Walmers upstairs, could not for the life of him help pausing at the room door, with, "I beg your pardon, sir, I hope you are not angry with Master Harry. For Master Harry's a fine boy, sir, and will do you credit and honour." Boots signifying while he related the circumstance, that "if the fine boy's father had contradicted him in the state of mind in which he then was, he should have 'fetched him a crack' and took the consequences."

As for the appreciation of Master Harry by the female dependents at the Holly Tree, there were two allusions to *that*—one general, as may be said, the other particular—that were always the most telling hits, the two chief successes of the Reading. Who that once heard it, for example, has forgotten the Author's inimitable manner of saying, as the Boots—" The way in which the women of that house—*without* exception—*every* one of 'em—married *and* single—took to that boy when they heard the story, is surprising. It was as much as could be done to keep 'em from dashing into the room and kissing him. They climbed up all sorts of places, at the risk of their lives, to look at him through a pane of glass. *They was seven deep at the key-hole!*" The climax of fun came naturally at the close, however, when, having described how Mr. Walmers lifted his boy up to kiss the sleeping "little warm face of little Mrs. Harry Walmers, junior," at the moment of their separation, Boots, that is the Reader, cried out in the shrill voice of one of the chambermaids, "*It's a shame to part 'em!*"

Two reflections indulged in by Boots during the course of his narrative, being among the pleasantest in connection with this most graceful of all the purely comic Readings, may here, while closing these allusions to it, be recalled to mind not inappropriately. One —where Cobbs "wished with all his heart there was any impossible place where them two babies could have made an impossible marriage, and have lived impossibly happy ever afterwards." The other—where, with genial sarcasm, Boots propounds this brace of opinions by way of general summing up—"Firstly, that there are not many couples on their way to be married who are half as innocent as them two children. Secondly, that it would be a jolly good thing for a great many couples on their way to be married, if they could only be stopped in time, and brought back separate." With which cynical scattering of sugar-plums in the teeth of married and single, the blithe Reading was laughingly brought to its conclusion.

BARBOX BROTHERS.

Nobody but the writer of this little freak of fancy could possibly have rendered the Reading of it in public worthy even of toleration. Perhaps no Reading that could be selected presents within the same compass so many difficulties to the audience who are listening, and to the Reader who is hardy enough to adventure upon its delivery. The closing incidents of the narrative are in themselves so improbable, we had all but said so impossible! Polly, at once so quaint and so captivating, when her words are perused upon the printed page, is so incapable of having her baby-prattle repeated by anybody else, without the imminent risk, the all but certainty, of its degenerating into mere childishness. It can scarcely be wondered, therefore, that "Barbox Brothers," though it actually was Read, and Read successfully, was hardly ever repeated. Everybody who has once looked into the story will bear in mind how, quite abruptly, almost haphazard, it comes to be narrated.

The lumbering, middle-aged, grey-headed hero of it,

in obedience to the whim of a moment, gets out of a night train at the great central junction of the whole railway system of England. A drenching rain-storm and a windy platform, darkness and solitude are, to begin with, the agreeable surroundings of this eccentric traveller. He is stranded there, not high and dry, anything but that—on the contrary, soaked through and through, and at very low level indeed—during what the local officials regard as their deadest time in all the twenty-four hours: what one of them, later on, terms emphatically their deadest and buriedest time.

Already, even here, before the tale itself is in any way begun, the Author of it, in his capacity as Reader, somehow, by the mere manner of his delivery of a descriptive sentence or two, contrived to realise to his hearers in a wonderfully vivid way the strange incidents of the traffic in a scene like this, at those blackest intervals between midnight and daybreak. Now revealing—"Mysterious goods trains, covered with palls, and gliding on like vast weird funerals, conveying themselves guiltily away, as if their freight had come to a secret and unlawful end." Now, again —"Half miles of coal pursuing in a Detective manner, following when they led, stopping when they stopped, backing when they backed." One while the spectacle, conjured up by a word or two was that of—"Unknown languages in the air, conspiring in red, green, and white characters." Another, with startling effect, it was—"An earthquake, with thunder and lightning, going up express to London." Here it is that Barbox Brothers, in the midst of these ghostly apparitions, is eventually extricated from the melancholy plight in which he finds himself saturated and isolated in the middle of a spiderous web of railroads.

His extricator is—Lamps! A worthy companion portrait to that of cinderous Mr. Toodles, the stoker, familiar to the readers of Dombey. Characters, those two, quite as typical, after their fashion, of the later railway period of Dickens, as even Sam Weller, the boots, and Old Weller, the coachman, were of his earlier coaching period in the days of Pickwick. To see him, in his capacity as Lamps, when excited, take what he called "a rounder"—that is to say, giving himself, with his oily handkerchief rolled up in the form of a ball, "an elaborate smear from behind the right ear, up the cheek, across the forehead, and down the other cheek, behind his left ear," after which operation he is described as having shone exceedingly—was to be with him, again, at once, in his greasy little cabin, which was suggestive to the sense of smell of a cabin in a whaler. How it came to pass that Lamps sang comic songs, of his own composition, to his bed-ridden daughter Phœbe, by way of enlivening her solitude, and how Phœbe, while manipulating the threads on her lace-pillow, as though she were playing a musical instrument, taught her little band of children to chant to a pleasant tune the multiplication-table, and so fix it and other useful knowledge indelibly upon the tablets of their memory, the Author-Reader would then relate, as no other Reader, however gifted, who was not also the Author, would have been allowed to do, supposing this latter had had the hardihood to attempt the relation.

As the Reading advanced, the difficulties not only increased, they became tenfold, immediately upon the introduction of Polly. Dickens, however, conquered them all somehow. But to anybody else, setting forth the story histrionically, impersonating the characters as they appeared, these difficulties would by necessity have been insuperable or simply overwhelming. Catching the very little fair-haired girl's Christian name readily enough, when she comes up to him in the street, with the surprising announcement, "O! if you please, I am lost!" Barbox Brothers can't for the life of him conjecture what her surname is,—carefully imitating, though he does, the sound that comes from the childish lips, each time on its repetition. Hazarding "Trivits," first of all, then "Paddens," then "Tappitarver." Eventually, when the two arrive hand-in-hand at Barbox Brothers' hotel, nobody there could make out her name as she set it forth, "except one chambermaid, who said it was Constantinople—which it wasn't."

No wonder Barbox feels bigger and heavier in person every minute when he is being catechised by Polly! Asked by her if he knows any stories, and compelled to answer, No! "What a dunce you must be, mustn't you?" says Polly. Frightened nearly out of his wits at the dinner-table, when they are feasting together, by her getting on her feet upon her chair to reward him with a kiss, and then toppling forward among the dishes—he himself crying out in dismay, "Gracious angels! Whew! I thought we were in the fire, Polly!"—"What a coward you are, ain't you?" says Polly, when replaced.

Upon the next morning, when brought down to breakfast, after a comfortable night's sleep, passed by the child in a bed shared with "the Constantinopolitan chambermaid," Polly, "by that time a mere heap of dimples," poses poor, unwieldy Barbox by asking him, in a wheedling manner, "What are we going to do, you dear old thing?" On his suggesting their having a sight, at the Circus, of two long-tailed ponies, speckled all over—"No, no, NO!" cries Polly, in an ecstasy. When he afterwards throws out a proposition that they shall also look in at the toy-shop, and choose a doll—"Not dressed," ejaculates Polly; "No, no, NO—not dressed!" Barbox replying, "Full dressed; together with a house, and all things necessary for housekeeping!" Polly gives a little scream, and seems in danger of falling into a swoon of bliss. "What a darling you are!" she languidly exclaims, leaning back in her chair: "Come and be hugged." All this will indicate plainly enough the difficulties investing every sentence of this Reading, capped as they all are by the astounding *denouement* of the plot—Polly turning out to be (sly little thing!) the purposely-lost daughter of Barbox Brothers' old love, Beatrice, and of her husband, Tresham, for whom Barbox had not only been jilted, but by whom Barbox had been simultaneously and rather heavily defrauded.

Perhaps the pleasantest recollection of the whole Reading is, not Polly — the small puss turns out to be such a cunningly reticent little emissary — but her Doll, a "lovely specimen of Circassian descent, possessing as much boldness of beauty as was reconcileable with extreme feebleness of mouth," and combining a sky-blue pelisse with rose-coloured satin trousers, and a black velvet hat, "the latter seemingly founded on the portraits of the late Duchess of Kent." One is almost reconciled to Polly, however,—becoming oblivious for the moment of her connivance in her mother's secret device, and reminiscent only of her own unsophisticated mixture of prattle and impertinence—on learning, immediately after this elaborate description of the gorgeous doll of her choice, that "the name of this distinguished foreigner was (on Polly's authority) Miss Melluka."

THE BOY AT MUGBY.

SEVERAL *gamins* have been contributed to our literature by Dickens—quite as typical and quite as truthful in their way, each of them, as Hugo's Gavroche. There is Jo the poor crossing-sweeper. There is the immortal Dodger. There is his pal the facetious Charley Bates. And there is that delightful boy at the end of "The Carol," who conveys such a world of wonder through his simple reply of "Why, Christmas Day!" The boy who is "as big," he says himself, as the prize turkey, and who gets off at last quicker than a shot propelled by the steadiest hand at a trigger! Scattered up and down the Boz fictions, there are abundant specimens of a *genus* that, in one instance, is actually termed by the Humorist, "a town-made little boy"—this is in the memorable street scene where Squeers hooks Smike by the coat-collar with the handle of his umbrella. He is always especially great in his delineation of what one might call the human cock-sparrows of London. Kit, at the outset of his career, is another example; and Tom Scott yet another.

Sloppy carries us away into the suburbs, thereby taking us in a manner off the stones, and otherwise represents in his own proper person, buttons and all, less one of the dapper urchins we are now more particularly referring to, than the shambling hobbledehoy. Even in the unfinished story with which the Author's voluminous writings were closed, there was portrayed an entirely novel specimen, one marked by the most grotesque extravagance, in the shape of that impish malignant, "the Deputy," whose pastime at once and whole duty in life seemed to be making a sort of vesper cock-shy of Durdles and his dinner-bundle.

Conspicuous among these comic boys of Dickens may be remembered one who, instead of being introduced in any of the Novelist's larger works, from the Pickwick Papers down to Edwin Drood, interpolates himself, as may be said, among one of the groups of Christmas stories, through the medium of a shrill monologue. "The Boy at Mugby," to wit, the one exhilarated and exhilarating appreciator of the whole elaborate system of Refreshmenting in this Isle of the Brave and Land of the Free, by which he means to say Britannia.

Laconically, "I am the Boy at Mugby," he announces. "That's about what *I* am." His exact location he describes almost with the precision of one giving latitude and longitude—explaining to a nicety where his stand is taken. "Up in a corner of the Down Refreshment Room at Mugby Junction," in the height of twenty-seven draughts [he's counted 'em, he tells us parenthetically, as they brush the First Class, hair twenty-seven ways], bounded on the nor'-west by the beer, and so on. He himself, he frankly informs you—in the event of your ever presenting yourself there before him at the counter, in quest of nourishment of any kind, either liquid or solid—will seem not to hear you, and will appear "in a absent manner to survey the Line through a transparent medium composed of your head and body," determined evidently not to serve you, that is, as long as you can possibly bear it! "That's me!" cries the Boy at Mugby, exultantly,—adding, with an intense relish for his occupation, "what a delightful lark it is!" As for the eatables and drinkables habitually set forth upon the counter, by what he generally speaks of as the Refreshmenters, quoth the Boy at Mugby, in a *naïf* confidence, addressed to you in your capacity at once as applicant and victim, "when you're telegraphed, you should see 'em begin to pitch the stale pastry into the plates, and chuck the sawdust sangwiches under the glass covers, and get out the—ha, ha!—the sherry—O, my eye, my eye!—for your refreshment." Once or twice in a way only, "The Boy at Mugby" was introduced among the Readings, and then merely as a slight stop-gap or interlude. Thoroughly enjoying the delivery of it himself, and always provoking shouts of laughter whenever this colloquial morsel was given, the Novelist seemed to be perfectly conscious himself that it was altogether too slight and trivial of its kind, to be worthy of anything like artistic consideration; that it was an "airy nothing" in its way, to which it was scarcely deserving that he should give more than name and local habitation.

Critically regarded, it had its inconsistencies too, both as a writing and as a Reading. There was altogether too much precocity for a genuine boy, in the nice discrimination with which the Boy at Mugby hit off the contrasting nationalities. The foreigner, for example, who politely, hat in hand, "beseeched Our Young Ladies, and our Missis," for a "leetel gloss hoff prarndee," and who, after being repelled, on trying to help himself, exclaims, "with hands clasped and shoulders riz: 'Ah! is it possible this; that these disdaineous females are placed here by the administration, not only to empoisen the voyagers, but to affront them! Great Heaven! How arrives it? The English people. Or is he then a slave? Or idiot?'" Hardly would a veritable boy, even an urchin so well "to the fore" with his epoch, as the Boy at Mugby, depict so accurately, much less take off, with a manner so entirely life-like, the astounded foreigner, any more than he would the thoroughly wide-awake and gaily derisive American. The latter he describes as alternately trying and spitting out first the sawdust and then the—ha, ha!—the sherry, until finally, on paying for both and consuming neither, he says, very loud, to Our Missis, and very good tempered, "I tell Yew what 'tis ma'arm. I la'af. Theer! I la'af, I Dew. I oughter ha' seen most things, for I hail from the Onlimited side of the Atlantic Ocean, and I haive travelled right slick over the Limited, head on, through Jeerusalem and the East, and likeways France and Italy, Europe, Old World, and I am now upon the track to the Chief Eurōpean Village; but such an Institution as Yew and Yewer fixins, solid *and* liquid, afore the glorious Tarnal I never did see yet! And if I hain't found the eighth wonder of Monarchical Creation, in finding Yew and Yewer fixins, solid *and* liquid, in a country where the people air not absolute Loo-naticks, I am Extra Double Darned with a nip and frizzle to the innermost grit! Wheerfore—Theer! —I la'af! I Dew, ma'arm. I la'af!" A calotype, or rather, literally, a speaking likeness, so true to the life as that, would be a trifle, we take it, beyond the mimetic powers and the keenly observant faculties even of a Boy whose senses had been wakened up by the twenty-seven cross draughts of the Refreshment Room at Mugby.

As to the fun made of the bandolining by Our Young Ladies, and of Our Missis's lecture on Foreign Refreshmenting, and of Sniff's corkscrew and his servile disposition, it is intentionally fooling, no doubt, but it is —excellent fooling! As was admirably said in the number of *Macmillan* for January, 1871, by the anonymous writer of a Reminiscence of the Amateur Theatricals at Tavistock House,—the remark following immediately after Charles Dickens's version of the Ghost's Song in Henry Fielding's burlesque of Tom Thumb,—"Nonsense, it may be said, all this; but the nonsense of a great genius has always something of genius in it." Had not Swift his "little language" to Stella, to "Stellakins," to "roguish, impudent, pretty M. D.?" Than some of which little language, quoth Thackeray, in commenting upon it, "I know of nothing more manly, more tender, more exquisitely touching." Again, had not Pope, in conjunction with the Dean, his occasional unbending also as a *farceur*, in the wilder freaks and oddities of Martinus Scriblerus? So was it here with one who was beyond all doubt, more intensely a Humorist than either, when he wrote or read such harmless sarcasms and innocent whimsicalities, as those alternately underlying, and overlaying the boyish fun of this juvenile Refreshmenter at Mugby Junction.

DOCTOR MARIGOLD.

Already mention has been made of the extraordinary care lavished, as a general rule, by the Novelist upon the preparation of these Readings before they were, each in turn, submitted for the first time to public scrutiny. A strikingly illustrative instance of this may be here particularised. It occurred upon the occasion of a purely experimental Reading of "Doctor Marigold," which came off privately, on the evening of the 18th of March, 1866, in the drawing-room of Charles Dickens's then town residence, in Southwick Place, Tyburnia. Including, among those present, the members of his own home circle, his entire audience numbered no more than ten persons altogether. Four, at any rate, of that party may be here identified, each of whom doubtless still bears the occasion referred to vividly in his remembrance, — Robert Browning the poet, Charles Fechter the actor, Wilkie Collins the novelist, and John Forster the historian of the Commonwealth. Even in private, Dickens had never Read "Doctor Marigold" until that evening. Often as he Read it afterwards, he never Read it with a more contagious air of exhilaration. He hardly ever, in fact, gave one of his almost wholly comic and but incidentally pathetic Readings *so* effectively. In every sentence there was a zest or relish that was irresistible. The volubility of the "poor chap in the sleeved-waistcoat" sped the Reading on with a rapidity quite beyond anticipation, when the time, which had been carefully marked at the commencement of the Reading, came to be notified at its conclusion. That the merest first rehearsal should have run off thus glibly seemed just simply incomprehensible. With the sense of this surprise still fresh upon us, the tentative Reading being at the time only a few seconds completed, everything was explained, however, by a half-whispered remark made, to the present writer, in passing, by the Novelist — made by him half-weariedly, yet half-laughingly—"There! If I have gone through that already to myself once, I have gone through it two—hundred—times!" It was not lightly or carelessly therefore, as may now be seen, that Charles Dickens, in his later capacity—not pen-in-hand, or through green monthly numbers, but standing at a reading-desk upon a public platform—undertook the office of a popular entertainer.

Resolved throughout his career as a Reader to acquit himself of those newly-assumed responsibilities to the utmost of his powers, to the fullest extent of his capabilities, both physical and intellectual, he applied his energies to the task, with a zeal that, it is impossible not to recognise now, amounted in the end to nothing less than (literally) self-sacrifice. But for the devotion of his energies thus unstintingly to the laborious task upon which he had adventured—a task involving in its accomplishment an enormous amount of rapid travelling by railway, keeping him for months together, besides, in one ceaseless whirl of bodily and mental excitement—his splendid constitution, sustained and strengthened as it was by his wholesome enjoyment of out-of-door life, and his habitual indulgence in bathing and pedestrianism, gave him every reasonable hope of reaching the age of an octogenarian.

Bearing in mind in addition to the wear-and-tear of the Readings in England and America, the nervous shock of that terrible railway accident at Staplehurst, on the 9th of June, 1865, the lamentable catastrophe of exactly five years afterwards to the very day, that of the 9th of June, 1870, becomes readily comprehensible. Because of his absorption in his task, however, all through, he was unconscious for the most part of the wasting influence of his labours, or, if he was so at all towards the close of his career, he was so, even then, only fitfully and at the rarest intervals. Precisely in the same way, it may be remarked, in rogard to those who watched his whole course as a Reader, that so facile and so pleasureable to himself, as well as to them, appeared to be the novel avocation which had come of late years to be alternated with his more accustomed toil as an author, that it rendered even the most observant amongst them unconscious in their turn of the disastrously exhausting influence of this unnatural blending together of two professions. A remorseful sense of this comes back upon us now, when it is all too late, in our remembrance of that remark made by the Novelist immediately after the Private Reading of "Doctor Marigold," a remark then regarded as simply curious and interesting, but now having about it an almost painful significance. Never was work more thoroughly or more conscientiously done, from first to last, than in the instance of these Readings.

In the minute elaboration of the care with which they were prepared, in the vivacity with which they were one and all of them delivered, in the punctuality with which, whirled like a shuttle in a loom, to and fro, hither and thither, through all parts of the United Kingdom and of the United States, the Reader kept, link by link, an immensely-lengthened chain of appointments, until the first link was broken suddenly at Preston—one can recognise at length the full force of those simple words uttered by him upon the occasion of his Farewell Reading, where he spoke of himself as "a faithful servant of the public, always imbued with a sense of duty to them, and always striving to do his best." Among the many radiant illustrations that have been preserved of how thoroughly he did his best, not the least brilliant in its way was this eminently characteristic Reading of "Doctor Marigold."

All through it, from the very beginning down to the very end of his Confidences, the Cheap Jack, in his belcher neckcloth and his sleeved-waistcoat with the mother-o'-pearl buttons, was there talking to us, as only he could talk to us, from the foot-board of his cart. He remained thus before us from his first mention of his own father having always consistently called himself Willum to the moment when little Sophy—the third little Sophy—comes clambering up the steps, and reveals that she at least is not deaf and dumb by crying out to him, "Grandfather!" As for the patter of Doctor Marigold, it is among the humorous revelations of imaginative literature. Hear him when he is perhaps the best worth listening to, when he is in his true rostrum, when his bluchers are on his native foot-board, and his name is, more intensely than ever, Doctor Marigold! Don't we all remember him there, for example, on a Saturday night in the market-place—"Here's a pair of razors that'll shave you closer than the board of guardians; here's a flat-iron worth its weight in gold; here's a frying-pan artificially flavoured with essence of beefsteaks to that degree that you've only got for the rest of your lives to fry bread and dripping in it and there you are replete with animal food; here's a genuine chronometer-watch, in such a solid silver case that you may knock at the door with it when you come home late from a social meeting, and rouse your wife and family and save up your knocker for the postman; and here's half a dozen dinner-plates that you may play the cymbals with to charm the baby when it's fractious. Stop! I'll throw you in another article, and I'll give you that, and it's a rolling-pin; and if the baby can only get it well into it's mouth when its teeth is coming, and rub the gums once with it, they'll come through double in a fit of laughter equal to being tickled." And so on, ringing the changes on a thousand wonderful conceits and whimsicalities that come tumbling out one after another in inexhaustible sequence and with uninterrupted volubility.

The very Prince of Cheap Jacks, surely, is this Doctor Marigold! And, more than that, one who makes good his claim to the title of wit, humorist, satirist, philanthropist, and philosopher.

As for his philosophic contentment, what can equal that as implied in his summing up of his own humble surroundings? "A roomy cart, with the large goods hung outside, and the bed slung underneath it when on the road; an iron-pot and a kettle, a fireplace for the cold weather, a chimney for the smoke, a hanging-shelf and a cupboard, a dog and a horse. What more do you want? You draw off on a bit of turf in a green lane or by the roadside, you hobble your old horse and turn him grazing, you light your fire upon the ashes of the last visitors, you cook your stew, and you wouldn't call the Emperor of France your father."

As for his wit, hear him describe—What? "Why, I'll tell you! It's made of fine gold, and it's not broke, though there's a hole in the middle of it, and it's stronger than any fetter that was ever forged. What else is it? I'll tell you. It's a hoop of solid gold wrapped in a silver curl-paper that I myself took off the shining locks of the ever-beautiful old lady in Threadneedle Street, London city. I wouldn't tell you so, if I hadn't the paper to show, or you mightn't believe it even of me. Now, what else is it? It's a man-trap, and a hand-cuff, the parish stocks and a leg-lock, all in gold and all in one. Now, what else is it? It's a wedding-ring!"

As for something far better than any mere taste of his skill as a satirist, see the whole of his delectable take off—in contradistinction to himself, the itinerant Cheap Jack—of the political Dear Jack in the public market-place.

As for his philanthropy, it is unobtrusively proclaimed by the drift of his whole narrative, and especially by two or three among the more remarkable of its closing incidents.

As for his powers as a humorist, they may be found there *passim*, being scattered broadcast all through his autobiographic recollections.

To those recollections are we not indebted for a whole gallery of inimitable delineations? The Cheap Jack's very dog, for instance, who had taught himself out of his own head to growl at any person in the crowd that bid as low as sixpence! Or Pickleson the giant, with a little head and less in it. Of whom, observes Doctor Marigold, "He was a languid young man, which I attribute to the distance betwixt his extremities." About whom, when a sixpence is given to him by Doctor Marigold, the latter remarks in a preposterous parenthesis, "(for he was kept as short as he was long!)" As for Dickens's high falsetto, when speaking in the person of this same Pickleson, with a voice that, as Doctor Marigold says, seemed to come from his eyebrows, it was only just a shade more excruciatingly ridiculous than his guttural and growling objurgations in the character of the giant's proprietor, the fe-rocious Mim.

With all his modest appetite for the simpler pleasures of existence, Doctor Marigold betrays in one instance, by the way, the taste of a *gourmet*. "I knocked up a beefsteak-pudding for one," he says, "with two kidneys, a dozen oysters, and a couple of mushrooms thrown in:" adding, with a fine touch of nature drawn from experience, "It's a pudding to put a man in good humour with everything, except the two bottom buttons of his waistcoat."

Incomparably the finest portion of all this wonderfully original sketch of Doctor Marigold, both in the Writing and in the Reading, was that in which the poor Cheap Jack is represented as going through his customary patter on the foot-board with his poor little Sophy—the first of the three Sophies, his own by birth, and not simply by adoption—the while she is slowly dying on his shoulder. Thackeray was right when he said of the humour of Dickens, "It is a mixture of love and wit." Laughter and tears, with him, lay very near—speaking of him as an author, we may say by preference—lie very near indeed together. It is in those passages in which they come in astonishingly rapid alternation, and at moments almost simultaneously, that he is invariably at his very best. The incident here alluded to is one of these more exquisite descriptions, and it was one, that, by voice and look and manner, he himself most exquisitely delineated. When the poor Cheap Jack, with Sophy holding round his neck, steps out from the shelter of the cart upon the foot-board, and the waiting crowd all set up a laugh on seeing them—"one chuckle-headed Joskin (that I hated for it) making a bid 'tuppence for her!'"—Doctor Marigold begins his tragi-comic allocution. It is sown thickly all through with the most whimsical of his conceits, but it is interrupted also here and there with infinitely pathetic touches of tenderness.

Fragmentary illustrations of either would but dimly shadow forth, instead of clearly elucidating, what is here meant in the recollection of those who can still recall this Reading of "Doctor Marigold" to their remembrance. Those who never heard it as it actually fell from the Author's lips, by turning to the original sketch, and running through that particular portion of it to themselves, may more readily conjecture than by the aid of mere piecemeal quotation, all that the writer of those riant and tearful pages would be capable of accomplishing by its utterance, bringing to its delivery, as he could, so many of the rarer gifts of genius, and so many also of the rarest accomplishments of art.

SIKES AND NANCY.

On Saturday, the 14th of November, 1868, there were assembled together in front of the great platform in St. James's Hall, Piccadilly, as fit audience, but few, somewhere about fifty of the critics, artists, and literary men of London. A card of invitation, stamped with a facsimile of the well-known autograph of Charles Dickens, and countersigned by the Messrs. Chappell and Company, had, with a witty significance, bidden them to that rendezvous for a "Private Trial of the Murder in Oliver Twist." The occasion, in point of fact, was a sort of experimental rehearsal of the last and most daring of all these vividly dramatic Readings by the popular Novelist.

Conscious himself that there was a certain amount of audacity in his adventuring thus upon a delineation so really startling in its character, he was not unnaturally desirous of testing its fitness for representation before the public, first of all in the presence of those who were probably the best qualified to pronounce a perfectly dispassionate opinion. It certainly appeared somewhat dubious at the first, that question as to the suitability for portrayal before mixed assemblages, of one of the most powerfully tragic incidents ever depicted by him in the whole range of his voluminous contributions to imaginative literature. The passages selected to this end from his famous story of Oliver Twist were those relating more particularly to the Murder of Nancy by Bill Sikes. A ghastlier atrocity than that murder could hardly be imagined. In the book itself, as will be remembered, the crime is painted as with a brush dipped in blood rather than pigment. The infamous deed is there described in language worthy of one of the greatest realists in fictitious narrative. Henri de Balzac, even in his more sanguinary imaginings, never showed a completer mastery of the horrible.

Remembering all this, and feeling perfectly assured at the same time, that the scene then about to be depicted by the Author in person, would most certainly lose nothing of its terror in the representation, the acknowledgment may here be made by the writer of these pages, that, on entering the Hall that evening, he was in considerable doubt as to what might be the result of the experiment. Compared with the size of the enormous building, the group of those assembled appeared to be the merest handful of an audience clustered together towards the front immediately below the platform of the orchestra. Standing at the back of this group, the writer recalls to mind, in regard to that evening, a circumstance plainly enough indicating how fully his own unexpressed uncertainty was akin to that of the Author-Reader himself. The circumstance, namely, that Charles Dickens, immediately on entering the hall, before taking his place at his reading-desk upon the platform, came round, and after exchanging a few words with him, uttered this earnest Aside,—"I want you to watch this particularly, for I am very doubtful about it myself!" Before that Experimental Reading was half over, however, all doubt upon the matter was utterly dissipated. In the powerful effect of it, the murder-scene immeasurably surpassed anything he had ever achieved before as an impersonator of his own creations. In its climax, it was as splendid a piece of tragic acting as had for many years been witnessed.

What, in effect, was Macready's comment upon it some months afterwards, when, with an especial eye to the great tragedian's opinion, "Sikes and Nancy" was given at Cheltenham? It was laconic enough, but it afforded a world of pleasure to the Author-Actor when his old friend—himself the hero of so many tragic triumphs—summed up his estimate, by saying, characteristically, "Two Macbeths!"

Four of the imaginary beings of the novel were introduced, or, it should rather be said, were severally produced before us as actual embodiments. Occasionally, during one of the earlier scenes, it is true that the gentle voice of Rose Maylie was audible, while a few impressive words were spoken there also at intervals by Mr. Brownlow. But, otherwise, the interlocutors were four, and four only: to wit—Nancy, Bill Sikes, Morris Bolter, otherwise Noah Claypole, and the Jew Fagin. Than those same characters no four perhaps in the whole range of fiction could be more widely contrasted. Yet, widely contrasted, utterly dissimilar, though they are, in themselves, the extraordinary histrionic powers of their creator, enabled him to present them to view, with a rapidity of sequence or alternation, so astonishing in its mingled facility and precision, that the characters themselves seemed not only to be before us in the flesh, but sometimes one might almost have said were there simultaneously. Each in turn as portrayed by him—meaning portrayed by him not simply in the book but by himself in person—was in its way a finished masterpiece.

Looking at the Author as he himself embodied these creations—Fagin, the Jew, was there completely, audibly, visibly before us, by a sort of transformation! Here, in effect—as several years previously in the midst of his impersonation of Wilmot in Lord Lytton's comedy of Not so Bad as we Seem, namely, where, in the garret, the young patrician affects for a while to be Edmund Curll the bookseller—the impersonator's very stature, each time Fagin opened his lips, seemed to be changed instantaneously. Whenever he spoke, there started before us—high-shouldered, with contracted chest, with birdlike claws, eagerly anticipating by their every movement the passionate words fiercely struggling for utterance at his lips—that most villainous old tutor of young thieves, receiver of stolen goods, and very devil incarnate: his features distorted with rage, his penthouse eyebrows (those wonderful eyebrows!) working like the antennæ of some deadly reptile, his whole aspect, half-vulpine, half-vulture-like, in its hungry wickedness.

Whenever *he* spoke, again, Morris Bolter—quite as instantly, just as visibly and as audibly—was there upon the platform. Listening to him, though we were all of us perfectly conscious of doing, through the Protean voice, and looking at him through the variable features of the Novelist, we somehow saw, no longer the Novelist, but—each time Noah Claypole said a word—that chuckle-headed, long-limbed, clownish, sneaking varlet, who is the spy on Nancy, the tool of Fagin, and the secret evil-genius of Sikes, hounding the latter on, as he does, unwittingly, to the dreadful deed of homicide.

As for the Author's embodiment of Sikes—the burly ruffian with thews of iron and voice of Stentor—it was only necessary to hear that infuriated voice, and watch the appalling blows dealt by his imaginary bludgeon in the perpetration of the crime, to realise the force, the power, the passion, informing the creative mind of the Novelist at once in the original conception of the character, and then, so many years afterwards, in its equally astonishing representation.

It was in the portrayal of Nancy, however, that the genius of the Author-Actor found the opportunity, beyond all others, for its most signal manifestation. Only that the catastrophe was in itself, by necessity so utterly revolting, there would have been something exquisitely pathetic in many parts of that affecting delineation. The character was revealed with perfect consistency throughout—from the scene of suppressed emotion upon the steps of London Bridge, when she is scared with the eltrich horror of her forebodings, down to her last gasping, shrieking apostrophes, to "Bill, dear Bill," when she sinks, blinded by blood, under the murderous blows dealt upon her upturned face by her brutal paramour.

Then, again, the horror experienced by the assassin afterwards! So far as it went, it was as grand a reprehension of all murderers as hand could well have penned or tongue have uttered. It had about it something of the articulation of an avenging voice not against Sikes only, but against all who ever outraged, or ever dreamt of outraging, the sanctity of human life. And it was precisely this which tended to sublimate an incident otherwise of the ghastliest horror into a homily of burning eloquence, the recollection of which among those who once saw it revealed through the lips, the eyes, the whole aspect of Charles Dickens will not easily be obliterated. The moral drawn from it—and there was this moral interpenetrating or impregnating the whole—became appreciable, it might even have been by Sikes himself, from the first moment the ruffian realised that the crime had been actually accomplished. It spoke trumpet-tongued from the very instant when he recoiled from "it!" Nancy no more, but thenceforth flesh and blood—"But such flesh, and so much blood!" Nevertheless, in that Experimental Reading of the 14th of November, 1868, the effect of all this appeared, in the estimation of the present writer, to have been in a great measure marred by the abruptness with which, almost the instant after the crime had been committed, the Reading was terminated. Sikes burnt upon the hearth the blood-stained weapon with which the murder had been perpetrated—was startled for a moment by the hair upon the end of the club shrinking to a light cinder and whirling up the chimney—and then, dragging the dog (whose very feet were bloody) after him, and locking the door, left the house. There, the Experimental Reading abruptly terminated.

It seemed not only insufficient, but a lost opportunity. Insomuch, that the writer, on the following day, remonstrated with the Novelist as earnestly as possible, urging him to append to the Reading as it then stood some fragmentary portion, at least, of the chapter descriptive of the flight, so that the remorseful horror of Sikes might be more fully realised. Of the reasonableness of this objection, however, Dickens himself was so wholly unconvinced, that, in the midst of his arguments against it, he wrote, in a tone of good-humoured indignation, "My dear fellow, believe me that no audience on earth could be held for ten minutes after the girl's death. Give them time, and they would be revengeful for having had such a strain put upon them. Trust me to be right. I stand there, and I know." Than this nothing could very well have been more strongly expressed, as indicative of the conclusion at which he had deliberately arrived.

So frankly open to conviction was he, nevertheless, that, not disdaining to defer to the judgment of another when his own had been convinced, the Reading was eventually, after all, lengthened out by a very remarkable addition. The printed copy of this fragment of Oliver Twist, artistically compacted together as "A Reading," has, appended to it, in blue ink, three pages of manuscript in the Novelist's familiar handwriting, in which, with a cunning mastery of all the powers of condensation, he has compacted together in a few sentences what he always gave with wonderful effect before the public, the salient incidents of the murderer's flight, ending with his own destruction, and even his dog's, from the housetop.

Nothing that could most powerfully realise to the audience the ruffian's sense of horror and abhorrence has been there overlooked. The ghastly figure follows him everywhere. He hears its garments rustling in the leaves. "If *he* stopped, *it* stopped. If *he* ran, *it* followed." Turning at times to beat the phantom off, though it should strike him dead, the hair rises on his head, and his blood stands still, for it has turned with him and is behind him! Throwing himself on his back upon the road—" At his head it stood, silent, erect, and still: a human gravestone with its epitaph in Blood."

What is as striking as anything in all this Reading, however—that is, in the Reading copy of it now lying before us as we write—is the mass of hints as to by-play in the stage directions for himself, so to speak, scattered up and down the margin. "Fagin raised his right hand, and shook his trembling forefinger in the air," is there, on p. 101, in print. Beside it, on the margin in MS., is the word "Action." Not a word of it was said. It was simply *done*. Again, immediately below that on the same page — Sikes' *loquitur*—" 'Oh! you haven't, haven't you?' passing a pistol into a more convenient pocket ['Action,' again, in MS. on the margin.] 'That's lucky for one of us—which one that is don't matter.' " Not a word was said about the pistol—the marginal direction was simply attended to. On the opposite page, in print, "Fagin laid his hand upon the bundle, and locked it in the cupboard. But he did not take his eyes off the robber for an instant." On the margin in MS., oddly but significantly underlined, are the words, "Cupboard Action." So again afterwards, as a rousing self-direction, one sees notified in manuscript, on p. 107, the grim stage direction, "Murder Coming."

As certainly as the "Trial from Pickwick" was the most laughter-moving of all the Readings, and as the "Story of Little Dombey," again, was the most pathetic, "Sikes and Nancy" was in all respects the most powerfully dramatic and, in the grand tragic force of it, in many ways, the most impressive and remarkable.

THE FAREWELL READING.

In recording the incident of his Farewell Reading, there comes back to us a yet later recollection of the great Novelist; and illustrating, as it does, his passionate love for the dramatic art, it may here be mentioned not inappropriately.

It relates simply to a remark suddenly made by him —and which had been suggested, so far as we can remember, by nothing we had been talking about previously—towards the close of our very last suburban walk together. Going round by way of Lambeth one afternoon in the early summer of 1870, we had skirted the Thames along the Surrey bank, had crossed the river higher up, and on our way back were returning at our leisure through Westminster; when, just as we were approaching the shadow of the old Abbey at Poet's Corner, under the roof-beams of which he was so soon to be laid in his grave, with a rain of tears and flowers, he abruptly asked—

"What do you think would be the realisation of one

of my most cherished day-dreams?" Adding, instantly, without waiting for any answer, "To settle down now for the remainder of my life within easy distance of a great theatre, in the direction of which I should hold supreme authority. It should be a house, of course, having a skilled and noble company, and one in every way magnificently appointed. The pieces acted should be dealt with according to my pleasure, and touched up here and there in obedience to my own judgment; the players as well as the plays being absolutely under my command. There," said he, laughingly, and in a glow at the mere fancy, "*that's* my day-dream!"

Dickens's delighted enjoyment, in fact, of everything in any way connected with the theatrical profession, was second only to that shown by him in the indulgence of the master-passion of his life, his love of literature.

The way in which he threw himself into his labours, as a Reader, was only another indication of his intense affection for the dramatic art. For, as we have already insisted, the Readings were more than simply Readings, they were in the fullest meaning of the words singularly ingenious and highly elaborated histrionic performances. And his sustained success in them during fifteen years altogether, and, as we have seen, through as many as five hundred representations, may be accounted for in the same way as his still more prolonged success, from the beginning of his career as a Novelist down to its very close, from the Pickwick Papers to Edwin Drood, otherwise, during an interval of four-and-thirty consecutive years, as the most popular author of his generation.

The secret of his original success, and of the long sustainment of it in each of these two careers—as Writer and as Reader—is in a great measure discoverable in this, that whatever powers he possessed he applied to their very uttermost. Whether as Author or as Impersonator, he gave himself up to his appointed task, not partially or intermittingly, but thoroughly and indefatigably.

His rule in life, in this way, he has himself clearly explained in the forty-second chapter of David Copperfield. What he there says about David's industry and perseverance, applies as directly to himself, as what he also relates in regard to his young hero's earlier toils as a parliamentary reporter, and his precocious fame as a writer of fiction. Speaking at once for David and for himself, he there writes for both or for either, "Whatever I have tried to do in life, I have tried with all my heart to do well; whatever I have devoted myself to, I have devoted myself to completely; in great aims and in small I have always been thoroughly in earnest. I have never believed it possible that any natural or improved ability can claim immunity from the companionship of the steady, plain, hard-working qualities, and hope to gain its end. There is no substitute for thorough-going, ardent, and sincere earnestness. Never to put one hand to anything on which I could throw my whole self; and never to affect depreciation of my work, whatever it was, I find now to have been my golden rules." What is there said applies far more recognisably to the real Charles Dickens than to the imaginary David Copperfield.

Attestations of the truth of this were discoverable, at every turn, in regard to his regular system, his constant method, nay, his minutest tricks of habit, so to speak, both as Reader and as Novelist. It was so when as an Author, for example, note was taken, now of his careful forecast of a serial tale on as many slips as there were to be green monthly numbers; now of his elaborately corrected and recorrected manuscripts; now of the proof-sheets lying about, for revision at any and every spare moment, during the month immediately before publication. Or, when, on the other hand, in his capacity as a Reader, regard was had to the scrupulous exactitude with which the seemingly trivial minutiæ of what one might call the mere accompaniments, were systematically cared for or methodised. Announced to read, for instance, for the first time in some town he had never before visited for that purpose, or in some building in which his voice had never before been raised, he would go down to the empty hall long before the hour appointed for the Reading, to take the bearings, as he would say, or, in other words, to familiarise himself with the place beforehand. His interest in his audience, again, was something delightful. He was hardly less keenly observant of them than they of him. Through a hole in the curtain at the side, or through a chink in the screen upon the platform, he would eagerly direct your attention to what never palled upon his own, namely, the effect of the suddenly brightened sea of faces on the turning up of the gas, immediately before the moment of his own appearance at the reading-desk.

The evening at length came for his very last appearance at that familiar little reading-desk, on Tuesday, the 15th of March, 1870, on the platform of the St. James's Hall, Piccadilly. The largest audience ever assembled in that immense building, the largest, as already intimated, that ever can be assembled there for purely Reading purposes, namely, when the orchestra and the upper end of the two side-galleries have necessarily to be barred or curtained off from the auditorium, were collected together there under the radiant pendants of the glittering ceiling, every available nook and corner, and all the ordinary gangways of the Great Hall being completely occupied. The money value of the house that night was £422. Crowds were unable to obtain admittance at the entrances in the Quadrant and in Piccadilly, long before the hour fixed for the Farewell Reading. Inside the building 2034 persons were seated there, eagerly awaiting the Novelist's appearance. The enthusiasm of his reception when eight o'clock came, and he advanced to the centre of the platform, of itself told plainly enough, as plainly as the printed bills announcing the fact in red, black, and yellow, that it was his last appearance.

The Readings selected were, as the very best that could have been chosen, his own favourites —"The Christmas Carol," and the "Trial from Pickwick." He never read better in his life than he did on that last evening. Evidently enough, he was nerved to a crowning effort. And by sympathy his audience—his last audience—responded to him throughout by their instant and intense appreciation. Not a point was lost. Every good thing told to the echo, that is, through the echoing laughter. Scrooge, Fezziwig, the Fiddler, Topper, every one of the Cratchits, everybody in "The Carol," including the Small Boy who is so great at repartee, all were welcomed in turn, as became them, with better than acclamations. It was the same exactly with the "Trial from Pickwick"—Justice Stareleigh, Serjeant Buzfuz, Mr. Winkle, Mrs. Cluppins, Sam Weller, one after another appearing for a brief interval, and then disappearing for ever, each of them a delightfully humorous, one of them in particular, the Judge, a simply incomparable impersonation.

Then came the moment of parting between the

great Author and his audience—that last audience who were there as the representatives of his immense public in both hemispheres. When the resounding applause that greeted the close of that Final Reading had died out, there was a breathless hush as Charles Dickens, who had for once lingered there upon the platform, addressed to his hearers, with exquisitely clear articulation, but with unmistakably profound emotion, these few and simple words of farewell:—

"Ladies and Gentlemen,—It would be worse than "idle, for it would be hypocritical and unfeeling, if I "were to disguise that I close this episode in my life "with feelings of very considerable pain. For some "fifteen years in this hall, and in many kindred places, "I have had the honour of presenting my own che-"rished ideas before you for your recognition, and in "closely observing your reception of them have en-"joyed an amount of artistic delight and instruction, "which perhaps it is given to few men to know. In "this task and in every other I have ever undertaken "as a faithful servant of the public, always imbued "with the sense of duty to them, and always striving "to do his best, I have been uniformly cheered by the "readiest response, the most generous sympathy, and "the most stimulating support. Nevertheless, I have "thought it well, at the full flood-tide of your favour, "to retire upon those older associations between us, "which date from much further back than these, and "thenceforth to devote myself exclusively to the art "that first brought us together. Ladies and gentle- "men, in two short weeks from this time I hope that "you may enter, in your own homes, on a new series "of readings at which my assistance will be indispen- "sable; but from these garish lights I vanish now for "evermore, with a heartfelt, grateful, respectful, and "affectionate farewell."

The manly, cordial voice only faltered once at the very last. The mournful modulation of it in the utterance of the words, "From these garish lights I vanish now for evermore," lingers to this moment like a haunting melody in our remembrance. Within a few weeks afterwards those very words were touchingly inscribed on the Funeral Card distributed at the doors of Westminster Abbey on the day of the Novelist's interment in Poet's Corner. As he moved from the platform after the utterance of the last words of his address and, with his head drooping in emotion, passed behind the screen on his way to his retiring-room, a cordial hand was placed for one moment with a sympathetic grasp upon his shoulder. The popularity won by Charles Dickens, even among the million who never saw him or spoke with him, amounted to nothing less than personal affection. Among his friends and intimates no great author has ever been more truly or more tenderly beloved. The prolonged thunder of applause that followed him to his secluded room at the back of the platform, whither he had withdrawn alone, recalled him after the lapse of some minutes for another instant into the presence of his last audience, from whom, with a kiss of his hand, he then indeed parted for evermore.

THE END.

BRADBURY, EVANS, AND CO., PRINTERS, WHITEFRIARS.

www.ingramcontent.com/pod-product-compliance
Lightning Source LLC
LaVergne TN
LVHW010225110826
845151LV00004B/1190

* 9 7 8 1 4 2 5 5 2 6 5 5 9 *